GREAT-TASTING

99¢

RECIPES

MONEY-SAVING MEALS

PUBLICATIONS INTERNATIONAL, LTD.

Pictured on the front cover *(clockwise from top right):* Lemon Chicken and Vegetables *(page 54),* Cheese and Bean Quesadillas *(page 44),* Homemade Pizza *(page 38)* and Lemon Pepper Chicken *(page 30).*
Pictured on the back cover: Stuffed Shells Florentine *(page 48).*

ISBN: 0-7853-2531-X

Manufactured in U.S.A.

8 7 6 5 4 3 2 1

Microwave Cooking: Microwave ovens vary in wattage. Use the cooking times as guidelines and check for doneness before adding more time.

GREAT-TASTING

99¢

RECIPES

MONEY-SAVING MEALS

$MART $hopping

Today, people everywhere are concerned with budgeting their money. Grocery shopping and meal planning are very important parts of saving money and sticking to a budget. With **99¢ Recipes and Money-Saving Meals** creating fabulous frugal meals for your family and friends has never been easier. Let us do the meal budgeting for you while you become your family's cost-cutting cook.

Every recipe in this collection has been individually priced to determine the cost per serving. Due to the varying cost of food items in different regions and during different seasons, each recipe does not have an exact price per serving. Each recipe is marked with the 99¢ or Less icon or the Budget Meal icon before the title.

 Per serving, this recipe does not cost more than 99¢ to make.

 Per serving, this recipe does not cost more than $1.50 to make.

- All food prices are based on a typical grocery store, excluding sale prices.

- The price of each recipe includes all the ingredients that are listed in the recipe, *except* water, salt, pepper and ingredients labeled as "dash," "to taste," "optional" or "for garnish."

- If a range is offered for an ingredient ("⅛ to ¼ teaspoon," for example), the *first* amount given was used to calculate the price per serving.

- If an ingredient is presented with an option ("¾ cup chopped tomatoes or red bell peppers," for example), the *first* item listed was used to calculate the price per serving.

- If a range is offered for servings ("Makes 4 to 6 servings," for example), the *last* amount given was used to calculate the price per serving.

- Foods shown in the photographs on the same serving plate and offered as "serve with" suggestions at the end of a recipe are *not* included in the pricing of the recipe except in cases where they are listed in the ingredient list.

CLIPPING COUPONS

Coupons *do* count! A few dollars a week might not seem like a lot, but the money you save by using coupons really adds up over the course of a year. File all your coupons in a convenient place where you will remember to bring them to the grocery store. Without your coupons in hand, they will do you no good.

SALE SAVVY

Take advantage of sales! Read the food section of your local newspaper and the weekly grocery store ads before you go shopping and stock up on items that can be stored. Canned goods, pasta and grains have a long shelf life; poultry, meat and butter freeze well. So if you have room, buying in bulk can be economical.

WRITE IT DOWN!

Make a grocery list before you go shopping; it will get you out of the store faster, and it will also prevent you from spending money on things you don't need.

MEAT MATTERS

While pre-cubed, pre-pounded or pre-seasoned meats (or poultry) can save you preparation time, they cost a lot more than plain cuts of meat. If you can spare a few minutes to cut, pound or season your meat, you'll find the savings are significant.

PRICING POULTRY

Dark meat costs less than white, so if your family likes dark meat, then you're in luck. Also, consider that the more work done to the poultry, the more it will cost you. If you have enough time to remove the skin from the poultry yourself, or if you will be cooking bone-in pieces instead of boneless, then the poultry you purchase will be less expensive. Look for family packs whenever possible, as the price per pound is much lower and it's very easy to repackage the poultry into cooking portions.

CONVENIENCE COSTS

Boneless chicken breasts are an example of a good timesaving investment, but snack-packs and lunch-size portions are not. If a convenience item significantly reduces your time and hassles in the kitchen, it's probably worth the cost. But anything that can be done quickly and easily at home, such as bagging small portions of chips and slicing cheese, will save you a lot of money.

A MATTER OF TASTE

Follow the basic rule of shopping: If your family won't eat it, don't buy it—at any price! Even if you're tempted by rock-bottom prices, these products will be no bargain if nobody likes them.

COST CUTTERS CHART

INSTEAD OF:	BUY:
packages of sliced or grated cheese	blocks of cheese
refrigerated cartons of fruit juice	frozen juice concentrate
quart-size cartons of milk	gallons or half-gallons of milk
loose fruit and vegetables by the pound	bagged produce, such as potatoes and apples
single-serving packages of snacks and cereal	family- or economy-sized packages
packaged vegetables for soups and stews	individual vegetables by the pound
small packages of nuts and dried fruits	bulk nuts and dried fruits sold by weight
brand-name grocery products	generic and store-brand products

MONEY–SAVING
Soups & Stews

Create the perfect one-pot meal. From soups and stews to chilis and chowders, you'll have a super selection to choose from. On chilly days, nothing hits the spot like a big bowl of hearty soup. With every piping hot spoonful of chunky vegetables, rich broth and savory meats, even a monster appetite will be satisfied. Ladle it up!

 **Potato-Bacon Soup**

Makes 4 servings

> 2 cans (about 14 ounces each) chicken broth
> 3 russet potatoes (1¾ to 2 pounds), peeled and cut into ½-inch cubes
> 1 medium onion, finely chopped
> 1 teaspoon dried thyme leaves
> 4 to 6 strips bacon (4 to 6 ounces), chopped
> ½ cup (2 ounces) shredded Cheddar cheese

1. Combine broth, potatoes, onion and thyme in Dutch oven; bring to a boil over high heat. Reduce heat to medium-high and boil 10 minutes or until potatoes are tender.

2. While potatoes are cooking, place bacon in microwavable container. Cover with paper towels and cook on HIGH 6 to 7 minutes or until bacon is crisp, turning after 3 minutes. Break up bacon.

3. Immediately transfer bacon to broth mixture with slotted spoon; simmer 3 to 5 minutes. Season to taste with salt and pepper. Ladle into bowls and sprinkle with cheese.

Prep and cook time: 27 minutes

Potato-Bacon Soup

Szechuan Vegetable Lo Mein

99¢ OR LESS Szechuan Vegetable Lo Mein

Makes 4 servings

2 cans (about 14 ounces each) vegetable or chicken broth
2 teaspoons bottled minced garlic
1 teaspoon bottled minced fresh ginger *or*
  ½ teaspoon ground ginger
¼ teaspoon red pepper flakes
1 package (5 ounces) Oriental curly noodles or
  5 ounces angel hair pasta, broken in half
1 package (16 ounces) frozen vegetable medley
  (broccoli, carrots, water chestnuts and red bell peppers)
3 tablespoons soy sauce
1 tablespoon dark sesame oil
¼ cup thinly sliced green onion tops

1. Combine broth, garlic, ginger and red pepper flakes in large deep skillet. Cover and bring to a boil over high heat.

2. Add noodles and vegetables to skillet; cover and return to a boil. Reduce heat to medium-low; simmer, uncovered, 5 to 6 minutes or until noodles and vegetables are tender, stirring occasionally.

3. Stir soy sauce and sesame oil into broth mixture; cook 3 minutes. Stir in green onions; ladle into bowls.

Prep and cook time: 20 minutes

Note: For a heartier, protein-packed main dish, add 1 package (10½ ounces) extra-firm tofu, cut into ¾-inch pieces, to the broth mixture with the soy sauce and sesame oil.

 # Spinach and Mushroom Soup

Makes 4 servings

1½ cups 1% milk
  3 medium potatoes, peeled and chopped (1 cup)
  1 box (10 ounces) BIRDS EYE® frozen Chopped Spinach
  1 can (10¾ ounces) cream of mushroom soup

- In large saucepan, heat milk and potatoes over medium-low heat 10 minutes.

- Add spinach and soup.

- Cook about 10 minutes or until soup begins to bubble and potatoes are tender, stirring frequently.

Prep time: 5 minutes
Cook time: 20 minutes

 # Italian Sausage and Vegetable Stew

Makes 6 (1-cup) servings

  1 pound hot or mild Italian sausage, cut into 1-inch pieces
  1 package (16 ounces) frozen mixed vegetables (onions and green, red and yellow peppers)
  2 medium zucchini, sliced
  1 can (14½ ounces) diced Italian-style tomatoes, undrained
  1 jar (4½ ounces) sliced mushrooms, drained
  4 cloves garlic, minced

1. Cook sausage in large saucepan, covered, over medium to medium-high heat 5 minutes or until browned; pour off drippings.

2. Add frozen vegetables, zucchini, tomatoes, mushrooms and garlic; bring to a boil. Reduce heat to low; simmer, covered, 10 minutes. Cook, uncovered, 5 to 10 minutes or until juices have thickened slightly.

Prep and cook time: 30 minutes

Serving Suggestion: Italian Sausage and Vegetable Stew is excellent served with garlic bread.

 # Creamy Asparagus Potato Soup

Makes 4 servings

  1 can (15 ounces) DEL MONTE® *FreshCut*™ Asparagus Spears, drained
  1 can (14½ ounces) DEL MONTE® *FreshCut*™ New Potatoes, drained
  ½ teaspoon dried thyme, crushed
  ⅛ teaspoon garlic powder
  1 can (14 ounces) chicken broth
  1 cup milk or half & half

1. Place asparagus, potatoes, thyme and garlic powder in food processor or blender (in batches, if needed); process until smooth.

2. Pour into medium saucepan; add broth. Bring to boil. Stir in milk; heat through. *(Do not boil.)* Season with salt and pepper to taste, if desired. Serve hot or cold. Thin with additional milk or water, if desired.

Prep time: 5 minutes
Cook time: 5 minutes

Smoked Sausage Gumbo

Makes 4 servings

¾ pound Polish or other smoked sausage
1 cup long-grain converted white rice
1 medium onion, diced
1 green bell pepper, diced
2 ribs celery, chopped
1 large carrot, peeled and chopped
2 teaspoons dried oregano leaves
2 teaspoons dried thyme leaves
⅛ teaspoon ground red pepper
¼ cup all-purpose flour
2 tablespoons olive oil
1 can (14½ ounces) diced tomatoes, undrained
1 can (about 14 ounces) chicken broth

1. Bring 2 cups water to a boil in medium saucepan over high heat. Meanwhile, cut sausage in half lengthwise, then crosswise into ½-inch slices.

2. Stir rice into boiling water. Reduce heat to low; cover and simmer 18 minutes or until liquid is absorbed.

3. While rice is cooking, place sausage, onion, bell pepper, celery, carrot, oregano, thyme and ground red pepper in large microwavable container. Cover and cook on HIGH 5 minutes; stir. Cook 3 minutes more or until vegetables are crisp-tender.

4. While vegetable mixture is cooking, prepare roux. Sprinkle flour evenly over bottom of Dutch oven. Cook over high heat, without stirring, 3 to 4 minutes or until flour begins to brown. Reduce heat to medium and stir flour about 4 minutes or until evenly browned. Stir in oil until smooth. (Roux will be thick and chocolate brown.)

5. Carefully pour vegetable mixture into Dutch oven and stir until coated with roux. Stir in tomatoes and broth; bring to a boil over high heat. Cover and simmer over medium heat 5 minutes. Serve gumbo over rice in individual bowls.

Prep and cook time: 30 minutes

For a special touch, sprinkle chopped parsley over each serving.

Note: If gumbo thickens upon standing, stir in additional broth.

Dijon Ham and Lentil Soup

Makes 6 servings

1 cup finely chopped onion
¾ cup finely chopped green bell pepper
½ cup finely chopped carrot
1 clove garlic, minced
1 bay leaf
2 (13¾-fluid ounce) cans chicken broth or lower
    sodium chicken broth
1 (14½-ounce) can stewed tomatoes
1¼ cups water
1 cup diced ham
¾ cup dry lentils
½ cup GREY POUPON® Country Dijon Mustard

In large saucepan, combine all ingredients except mustard. Heat to a boil over medium-high heat. Reduce heat; simmer, uncovered, for 1 hour. Stir in mustard. Serve hot.

Smoked Sausage Gumbo

 **Beer and Cheese Soup**

Makes 6 (1-cup) servings

2 to 3 slices pumpernickel or rye bread
3 tablespoons cornstarch
¼ cup finely chopped onion
1 tablespoon butter or margarine
¾ teaspoon dried thyme leaves
2 cloves garlic, minced
1 can (about 14 ounces) chicken broth
1 cup beer
1½ cups (6 ounces) shredded or diced American cheese
1 cup (4 ounces) shredded sharp Cheddar cheese
½ teaspoon paprika
1 cup 2% milk

1. Preheat oven to 425°F. Slice bread into ½-inch cubes; place on baking sheet. Bake 10 to 12 minutes, stirring once, or until crisp; set aside.

2. While bread is in oven, stir 3 tablespoons water into cornstarch in small bowl; set aside. Place onion, butter, thyme and garlic in 3-quart saucepan; cook and stir over medium-high heat 3 to 4 minutes or until onion is tender. Add broth; bring to a boil. Stir in beer, cheeses and paprika. Reduce heat to low; whisk in milk and cornstarch mixture. Stir until cheese melts and soup bubbles and thickens. Ladle into bowls. Top with croutons.

Prep and cook time: 20 minutes

 **Skillet Sausage and Bean Stew**

Makes 4 servings

1 pound spicy Italian sausage, casing removed and sliced ½ inch thick
½ onion, chopped
2 cups frozen O'Brien-style potatoes with onions and peppers
1 can (15 ounces) pinto beans, undrained
1 teaspoon beef bouillon granules or 1 beef bouillon cube
1 teaspoon dried oregano leaves
⅛ teaspoon ground red pepper

1. Combine sausage slices and onion in large nonstick skillet; cook and stir over medium-high heat 5 to 7 minutes or until meat is no longer pink. Drain drippings.

2. Stir in potatoes, beans, ¾ cup water, bouillon, oregano and red pepper; reduce heat to medium. Cover and simmer 15 minutes, stirring occasionally.

Prep and cook time: 30 minutes

Lighten Up: You can reduce the calories and fat content of this dish by substituting turkey sausage for Italian sausage. Add hot pepper sauce to taste if you prefer a spicier stew.

Beer and Cheese Soup

 **Middle Eastern Lentil Soup**

Makes 4 servings

1 cup dried lentils
2 tablespoons olive oil
1 onion, chopped
1 red bell pepper, chopped
1 teaspoon fennel seed
½ teaspoon ground cumin
¼ teaspoon ground red pepper
½ teaspoon salt
1 tablespoon lemon juice
Fresh parsley
½ cup plain yogurt

1. Rinse lentils, discarding any debris or blemished lentils; drain.

2. Heat oil in large saucepan over medium-high heat until hot. Add onion and bell pepper; cook and stir 5 minutes or until tender. Add fennel seed, cumin, and ground red pepper; cook and stir 1 minute.

3. Add 4 cups water and lentils. Bring to a boil. Reduce heat to low. Cover and simmer 20 minutes. Stir in salt. Simmer 5 to 10 minutes more or until lentils are tender. Refrigerate, covered, overnight or up to 2 days.

4. To complete recipe, reheat soup over medium heat until hot. Stir in lemon juice.

5. While soup is reheating, chop enough parsley to measure 2 tablespoons; stir into yogurt. Serve soup topped with yogurt mixture.

Make-ahead time: up to 2 days before serving
Final prep time: 10 minutes

For a special touch, top each serving with yellow bell pepper strips.

 **Tuna Corn Chowder**

Makes 2 servings

2 strips bacon
1 small onion
2 ribs celery, chopped
1½ tablespoons all-purpose flour
2 cups 2% milk
½ teaspoon dried thyme leaves
¼ teaspoon salt
¼ teaspoon pepper
1 cup frozen whole kernel corn
1 can (6 ounces) tuna packed in water, drained

1. Cook bacon in large saucepan over medium-high heat until browned and crisp, turning once. Drain on paper towels, reserving drippings in saucepan.

2. Add onion and celery to pan drippings; cook and stir over medium-high heat 3 minutes or until softened.

3. Add flour, stirring until well blended; cook 1 minute. Stir in milk, thyme, salt and pepper. Cook, stirring frequently, until thickened.

4. Stir in corn and tuna; cook over medium heat 5 minutes or until corn is tender, stirring frequently.

5. Crumble bacon. Serve chowder sprinkled with bacon.

Prep and cook time: 25 minutes

For a special touch, top chowder with red bell pepper strips or popped popcorn.

Albóndigas

 Albóndigas

Makes 6 servings

    1 pound lean ground beef
    ½ small onion, finely chopped
    1 egg
    ¼ cup dry bread crumbs
    1 tablespoon chili powder
    1 teaspoon ground cumin
    ½ teaspoon salt
    3 cans (about 14 ounces each) chicken broth
    1 medium carrot, thinly sliced
    1 package (10 ounces) frozen corn or thawed frozen
        leaf spinach
    ¼ cup dry sherry

1. Mix ground beef, onion, egg, bread crumbs, chili powder, cumin and salt in medium bowl until well blended. Place mixture on lightly oiled cutting board; pat evenly into 1-inch-thick square. Cut into 36 squares with sharp knife; shape each square into a ball.

2. Place meatballs slightly apart in single layer in microwavable container. Cover and cook on HIGH 3 minutes or until meatballs are no longer pink (or just barely pink) in center.

3. While meatballs are cooking, bring broth and carrot to a boil in covered Dutch oven over high heat. Stir in corn and sherry. Transfer meatballs to broth with slotted spoon. Reduce heat to medium and simmer 3 to 4 minutes or until meatballs are cooked through. (Stir in spinach, if using, and simmer until heated through.)

Prep and cook time: 30 minutes

For a special touch, sprinkle soup with chopped fresh cilantro.

20-Minute White Bean Chili

Makes 6 servings

- 1 cup chopped onions
- 1 clove garlic, minced
- 1 tablespoon vegetable oil
- 1 pound ground turkey
- 1 cup chicken broth or lower sodium chicken broth
- 1 (14½-ounce) can stewed tomatoes
- ⅓ cup GREY POUPON® Dijon Mustard
- 1 tablespoon chili powder
- ⅛ to ¼ teaspoon ground red pepper
- 1 (15-ounce) can cannellini beans, drained and rinsed
- 1 (8-ounce) can corn, drained
  Tortilla chips, shredded Cheddar cheese and cilantro, optional

In 3-quart saucepan, over medium-high heat, sauté onions and garlic in oil until tender. Add turkey; cook until done, stirring occasionally to break up meat. Drain. Stir in chicken broth, tomatoes, mustard, chili powder and pepper. Heat to a boil; reduce heat. Simmer for 10 minutes. Stir in beans and corn; cook for 5 minutes. Top with tortilla chips, shredded cheese and cilantro, if desired.

20-Minute White Bean Chili

Spicy Vegetable Stew

Makes 4 servings

- 1 tablespoon vegetable oil
- 2 carrots, chopped
- ½ onion, chopped
- 2 cloves garlic, minced
- 1 teaspoon ground cumin
- 1 teaspoon paprika
- ¾ teaspoon ground cinnamon
- ½ teaspoon salt
- ½ teaspoon ground ginger
- ½ teaspoon black pepper
- 1 can (14½ ounces) diced tomatoes
- 1 can (about 14 ounces) vegetable broth
- 1 cup frozen hash brown potatoes
- 1 cup frozen green beans
- 2 tablespoons tomato paste
- ¼ to ½ teaspoon hot pepper sauce
- 1⅓ cups uncooked couscous

1. Heat oil in large saucepan over medium-high heat until hot. Add carrots, onion, garlic, cumin, paprika, cinnamon, salt, ginger and pepper; cook and stir about 5 minutes or until vegetables are tender.

2. Stir in tomatoes, broth, potatoes, green beans, tomato paste and hot pepper sauce; bring to a boil. Reduce heat to low and simmer, uncovered, 10 minutes.

3. While stew is simmering, prepare couscous. Bring 1⅓ cups water to a boil in small saucepan over high heat. Stir in couscous. Cover and remove saucepan from heat; let stand 5 minutes.

4. Fluff couscous with fork. Serve vegetable stew over couscous.

Prep and cook time: 23 minutes

For a special touch, garnish with fresh Italian parsley.

99¢ OR LESS Hearty Pasta and Chick-Pea Chowder

Makes 6 servings (about 7 cups)

  6 ounces uncooked rotini pasta
  2 tablespoons olive oil
  ¾ cup chopped onion
  ½ cup chopped celery
  ½ cup thinly sliced carrot
  2 cloves garlic, minced
  ¼ cup all-purpose flour
  1½ teaspoons Italian seasoning
  ⅛ teaspoon crushed red pepper
  ⅛ teaspoon black pepper
  2 cans (about 14 ounces each) chicken broth
  1 can (19 ounces) chick-peas, rinsed and drained
  1 can (14½ ounces) Italian-style stewed tomatoes, undrained
  6 slices bacon

1. Cook rotini according to package directions. Rinse, drain and set aside.

2. Meanwhile, heat oil in 4-quart Dutch oven over medium-high heat until hot. Add onion, celery, carrot and garlic. Reduce heat to medium; cook and stir 5 to 6 minutes or until vegetables are crisp-tender.

3. Remove from heat. Stir in flour, Italian seasoning, crushed red pepper and black pepper until well blended. Gradually stir in broth. Return to heat and bring to a boil, stirring frequently. Boil, stirring constantly, 1 minute. Reduce heat to medium. Stir in cooked pasta, chick-peas and tomatoes. Cook 5 minutes or until heated through.

4. Meanwhile, place bacon between double layer of paper towels on paper plate. Microwave on HIGH 5 to 6 minutes or until bacon is crisp. Drain and crumble.

5. Sprinkle each serving with bacon. Serve immediately.

Prep and cook time: 30 minutes

Serving Suggestion: Top with grated Parmesan cheese and serve with crusty bread, salad greens tossed with Italian dressing and fruit cobbler.

BUDGET MEAL Brunswick Stew

Makes 4 (1-cup) servings

  12 ounces smoked ham or cooked chicken breast, cut into ¾- to 1-inch cubes
  1 cup sliced onion
  4½ teaspoons all-purpose flour
  2 cups frozen mixed vegetables for soup (okra, lima beans, potatoes, celery, corn, carrots, green beans and onions)
  1 can (14½ ounces) stewed tomatoes, undrained
  1 cup chicken broth

1. Spray large saucepan with nonstick cooking spray; heat over medium heat until hot. Add ham and onion; cook 5 minutes or until ham is browned. Stir in flour; cook over medium to medium-low heat 1 minute, stirring constantly.

2. Stir in remaining ingredients; bring to a boil. Reduce heat to low; simmer, covered, 5 to 8 minutes or until vegetables are tender. Simmer, uncovered, 5 to 8 minutes or until slightly thickened. Season to taste with salt and pepper.

Prep and cook time: 30 minutes

Serving Suggestion: Brunswick Stew is excellent served over rice or squares of cornbread.

Hearty Pasta and Chick-Pea Chowder

 **Creamy Groundnut Soup**

Makes 6 servings

- 1 jar (18 ounces) creamy or chunky peanut butter
- 1 can (about 14 ounces) chicken broth
- 2 cups milk
- 2 teaspoons bottled minced garlic
- 1½ teaspoons ground cumin
- ¼ teaspoon black pepper
- ¼ teaspoon ground red pepper
- 1 cup uncooked white rice

1. Combine peanut butter, chicken broth, milk, garlic, cumin, black pepper and red pepper in medium saucepan. Cook over low heat about 10 minutes, stirring frequently to blend. At this point, soup may be chilled up to 2 days.

2. To complete recipe, bring 2 cups water to a boil in small saucepan. Add rice; cover and simmer about 18 minutes or until rice is tender and water is absorbed.

3. While rice is cooking, heat soup in microwave on HIGH about 6 minutes or until hot, stirring occasionally. Top each bowl of soup with scoop of hot cooked rice.

Make-ahead time: up to 2 days before serving
Final prep and cook time: 25 minutes

For a special touch, top each serving with shredded carrot and thin mango slices.

 **Veggie Soup**

Makes 4 servings

- 1 bag (16 ounces) BIRDS EYE® frozen Mixed Vegetables
- 1 can (10 ounces) French onion soup
- 1 can (11 ounces) tomato rice soup
- 1 soup can of water

• In large saucepan, cook vegetables according to package directions; drain.

• Add both cans of soup and water; cook over medium-high heat until heated through.

Prep time: 2 minutes
Cook time: 10 to 12 minutes

Serving Suggestion: Sprinkle individual servings evenly with 1 cup shredded Cheddar cheese.

Veggie Soup

 Chili Stew

Makes 4 servings

  1 box (10 ounces) BIRDS EYE® frozen Sweet Corn
  2 cans (15 ounces each) chili
  1 can (14 ounces) stewed tomatoes
    Chili powder

• In large saucepan, cook corn according to package directions; drain.

• Stir in chili and tomatoes; cook until heated through.

• Stir in chili powder to taste.

Prep time: 2 minutes
Cook time: 7 to 10 minutes

Serving Suggestion: Serve with your favorite corn bread or sprinkle with shredded Cheddar cheese.

 Blender Potato Soup

Makes 8 servings

  ½ cup WESSON® Vegetable Oil
  3 cups chopped celery
1½ cups chopped onions
  1 teaspoon fresh minced garlic
  1 quart chicken broth
  3 cups peeled and diced russet potatoes
  ½ cup chopped fresh parsley, divided
  ½ teaspoon salt
  ¼ teaspoon pepper
    Shredded sharp Cheddar cheese

In a large saucepan, heat Wesson Oil. Add celery, onions and garlic; sauté until tender. Stir in *remaining* ingredients *except* ⅓ *cup* parsley and cheese; bring to a boil and reduce heat. Simmer, covered, for 20 minutes or until potatoes are tender. Pour *half* of mixture into blender; purée until smooth. Set aside. Pour *remaining* soup into blender; blend until coarsely chopped. Combine both mixtures. Ladle soup into bowls; garnish with *remaining* parsley and cheese.

 "Secret Chowder"

Makes 4 servings

  1 bag (16 ounces) BIRDS EYE® frozen Pasta Secrets
    White Cheddar
  1 can (10¾ ounces) cream of potato soup
  1 cup 1% milk
  ½ cup water
  ½ cup cubed cooked lean ham
  ½ teaspoon dried basil

• In medium saucepan, combine all ingredients.

• Bring to boil over medium-high heat. Reduce heat to medium; cook 15 minutes or until heated through. Add salt and pepper to taste.

Prep time: 5 minutes
Cook time: 15 minutes

Cheddar Cheese Chowder: Substitute 1 can Cheddar cheese soup for the cream of potato soup.

Minestrone Soup

Makes 4 to 6 servings

¾ cup small shell pasta
2 cans (about 14 ounces each) vegetable broth
1 can (28 ounces) crushed tomatoes in tomato purée
1 can (15 ounces) white beans, drained and rinsed
1 package (16 ounces) frozen vegetable medley
    (broccoli, green beans, carrots and red peppers)
4 to 6 teaspoons prepared pesto

1. Bring 4 cups water to a boil in large saucepan over high heat. Stir in pasta; cook 8 to 10 minutes or until tender. Drain.

2. While pasta is cooking, combine broth, tomatoes and beans in Dutch oven. Cover and bring to a boil over high heat. Reduce heat to low; simmer 3 to 5 minutes.

3. Add vegetables to broth mixture and return to a boil over high heat. Stir in pasta. Ladle soup into bowls; spoon about 1 teaspoon pesto in center of each serving.

Prep and cook time: 20 minutes

Minestrone Soup

 **All-in-One Burger Stew**

Makes 6 servings

1 pound lean ground beef
2 cups frozen Italian vegetables
1 can (14½ ounces) chopped tomatoes with basil and garlic
1 can (about 14 ounces) beef broth
2½ cups uncooked medium egg noodles

1. Cook meat in Dutch oven or large skillet over medium-high heat until no longer pink, breaking meat apart with wooden spoon. Drain drippings.

2. Add vegetables, tomatoes and broth; bring to a boil over high heat.

3. Add noodles; reduce heat to medium. Cover and cook 12 to 15 minutes or until noodles have absorbed liquid and vegetables are tender. Add salt and pepper to taste.

Prep and cook time: 25 minutes

For a special touch, sprinkle with chopped parsley before serving.

 **Thai Noodle Soup**

Makes 4 servings

1 package (3 ounces) ramen noodles
¾ pound chicken tenders
2 cans (about 14 ounces each) chicken broth
¼ cup shredded carrot
¼ cup frozen snow peas
2 tablespoons thinly sliced green onion tops
½ teaspoon bottled minced garlic
¼ teaspoon ground ginger
3 tablespoons chopped cilantro
½ lime, cut into 4 wedges

1. Break noodles into pieces. Cook noodles according to package directions, discarding flavor packet. Drain and set aside.

2. Cut chicken tenders into ½-inch pieces. Combine chicken broth and chicken tenders in large saucepan or Dutch oven; bring to a boil over medium heat. Cook 2 minutes.

3. Add carrot, snow peas, green onion, garlic and ginger. Reduce heat to low; simmer 3 minutes. Add cooked noodles and cilantro; heat through. Serve soup with lime wedges.

Prep and cook time: 15 minutes

For a special touch, garnish soup with green onion curls.

 **Clam Chowder**

Makes 4 servings

1 bag (16 ounces) BIRDS EYE® frozen Small Whole Onions
1 can (14 ounces) vegetable broth
2 cans (10 ounces each) clam chowder

• In large saucepan, place onions and broth; bring to boil over high heat. Reduce heat to medium; cover and simmer 7 to 10 minutes or until onions are tender.

• Stir in clam chowder; cook until heated through.

Prep time: 1 minute
Cook time: 10 to 12 minutes

All-in-One Burger Stew

CENTSIBLE
Simple Suppers

Dinner in a snap! When time is of the essence, serve up Garden Omelets bursting with fresh vegetables and gooey cheese, Zesty Lemon Pepper Chicken or Antipasto Salad Stack piled high with rotini pasta, spicy pepperoni, crispy lettuce and much more. It's easy to make all your simple suppers simply delicious.

Santa Fe Black Beans & Rice Salad

Makes 6 cups

½ cup GREY POUPON® Dijon Mustard
2 tablespoons REGINA® White Wine Vinegar
2 tablespoons olive oil
1 tablespoon chopped cilantro
1½ teaspoons liquid hot pepper seasoning
½ teaspoon chili powder
¼ teaspoon ground cumin
3 cups cooked long grain and wild rice
1 (15-ounce) can black beans, rinsed and drained
1 cup chopped tomato
1 cup canned corn
⅓ cup chopped red onion
¼ cup diced green chiles

In small bowl, blend mustard, vinegar, oil, cilantro, hot pepper seasoning, chili powder and cumin; set aside.

In large bowl, combine rice, beans, tomato, corn, onion and chiles. Add mustard mixture, tossing to coat well. Chill at least 1 hour before serving. Garnish as desired.

Santa Fe Black Beans & Rice Salad

 ## Pasta Niçoise

Makes 6 servings

12 ounces uncooked rotini
1 bottle (8 ounces) Italian vinaigrette
1 can (6 ounces) tuna packed in water, drained
3 eggs, hard boiled, peeled and cut into wedges
1 cup frozen green beans, thawed
¼ cup pitted black olives

1. Cook pasta according to package directions; drain.

2. Reserve ¼ cup vinaigrette. Toss pasta with remaining vinaigrette; place in serving bowl or on individual plates.

3. Arrange tuna, eggs, green beans and olives on top of pasta. Drizzle with reserved vinaigrette. Serve chilled or at room temperature.

Prep and cook time: 20 minutes

 ## Mediterranean Carrots with Chicken

Makes 4 servings

2 boxes (10 ounces each) BIRDS EYE® frozen Deluxe Baby Whole Carrots
2 cups cubed, cooked chicken breast
3 tablespoons brown sugar
2 tablespoons lemon juice
1 teaspoon cumin

• In large saucepan, combine all ingredients. Cover; cook over medium-low heat 20 minutes or until heated through and carrots are tender.

Prep time: 5 minutes
Cook time: 20 minutes

 ## Lemon Pepper Chicken

Makes 4 servings

⅓ cup lemon juice
¼ cup olive oil
¼ cup finely chopped onion
3 cloves garlic, minced
1 tablespoon cracked black pepper
1 tablespoon brown sugar
2 teaspoons grated lemon peel
¾ teaspoon salt
4 chicken quarters (about 2½ pounds)

COMBINE lemon juice, oil, onion, garlic, pepper, sugar, lemon peel and salt in small bowl; reserve 2 tablespoons marinade. Combine remaining marinade and chicken in large resealable plastic food storage bag. Seal bag; knead to coat. Refrigerate 4 hours or overnight.

REMOVE chicken from marinade; discard marinade. Arrange chicken on microwavable plate; cover with waxed paper. Microwave at HIGH 5 minutes. Turn and rearrange chicken. Cover and microwave at HIGH 5 minutes.

TRANSFER chicken to grill. Grill covered over medium-hot coals 15 to 20 minutes or until chicken is no longer pink in center and juices run clear, turning several times and basting often with reserved marinade.

Serving Suggestion: Serve with a mixed green salad and fresh lemon slices.

Lemon Pepper Chicken

Veggie Kabobs with Tex-Mex Polenta

Garden Omelet

Makes 2 servings

 3 teaspoons butter or margarine, divided
 ⅓ cup chopped onion
 ⅓ cup chopped red bell pepper
 ½ cup sliced mushrooms
 ½ teaspoon dried basil leaves
 4 eggs, beaten
 1 tablespoon milk
 ¼ teaspoon black pepper
   Dash salt
 ½ cup (2 ounces) shredded Swiss cheese

1. Melt 1 teaspoon butter in large nonstick skillet over medium heat. Cook and stir onion and bell pepper 2 to 3 minutes or until onion is tender. Add mushrooms and basil; cook and stir 3 to 5 minutes more. Remove vegetables from skillet and keep warm.

2. Whisk together eggs, milk, pepper and salt in medium bowl. Melt remaining 2 teaspoons butter in same skillet over medium heat; rotate pan to coat bottom. Pour egg mixture into skillet. Cook over medium heat; as eggs begin to set, gently lift edges of omelet with spatula and tilt skillet so that uncooked portion flows underneath.

3. When eggs are fully cooked, spoon vegetable mixture over half of omelet. Sprinkle with cheese. Loosen omelet with spatula and fold in half. Transfer to warm serving plate.

Prep and cook time: 20 minutes

 **Veggie Kabobs with Tex-Mex Polenta**

Makes 4 to 6 servings

POLENTA
2¾ cups water
¾ cup yellow cornmeal
½ teaspoon salt
1 can (4 ounces) chopped green chilies, drained
½ cup (2 ounces) shredded Monterey Jack cheese
2 tablespoons shredded Cheddar cheese
2 tablespoons grated Parmesan cheese

VEGGIE KABOBS
½ cup olive oil
¼ cup cider vinegar
1 teaspoon salt
¾ teaspoon garlic powder
½ teaspoon black pepper
3 large bell peppers, cut into 1½-inch pieces
1 medium red onion, cut into 1-inch wedges
8 ounces fresh mushrooms

1. Combine water, cornmeal and salt in large microwavable bowl. Cover tightly; microwave on HIGH 10 to 12 minutes, stirring halfway through cooking time. Stir in chilies and Monterey Jack cheese. Cover; let stand 2 minutes. Grease 9-inch casserole. Spread cornmeal mixture into prepared casserole. Cover; refrigerate 2 hours or until firm.

2. Preheat broiler. Turn polenta out of casserole; cut into 6 wedges. Grease small baking sheet. Place polenta on baking sheet. Broil 6 inches from heat 5 to 6 minutes per side. Sprinkle with Cheddar and Parmesan cheeses.

3. Soak 8 to 10 wooden skewers in water. Combine oil, vinegar, salt, garlic powder and pepper in medium bowl. Alternately thread bell peppers, onion and mushrooms onto skewers. Arrange skewers in shallow pan. Pour oil marinade over skewers. Cover; refrigerate at least 2 hours or overnight.

4. To complete recipe, preheat broiler. Transfer skewers to large baking sheet. Broil 8 to 10 minutes or until vegetables begin to brown. Serve with polenta.

Make-ahead time: 2 hours to 1 day before serving
Final prep and cook time: 22 minutes

 **Carpaccio di Zucchini**

Makes 4 servings

¾ pound zucchini, shredded
½ cup sliced almonds, toasted
1 tablespoon Italian salad dressing
4 French bread baguettes, sliced in half lengthwise
4 teaspoons soft spread margarine
3 tablespoons grated Parmesan cheese

1. Preheat broiler. Place zucchini in medium bowl. Add almonds and dressing; mix well. Set aside.

2. Place baguette halves on large baking sheet; spread evenly with margarine. Sprinkle with cheese. Broil 3 inches from heat 2 to 3 minutes or until edges and cheese are browned.

3. Spread zucchini mixture evenly on each baguette half. Serve immediately.

Prep and cook time: 28 minutes

For a special touch, garnish carpaccio with cherry tomato halves.

99¢ OR LESS Hot Crab and Cheese on Muffins

Makes 8 servings

4 English muffins, split
1 tablespoon butter or margarine
3 green onions, chopped
⅓ cup chopped red bell pepper
½ pound fresh crabmeat, drained and flaked*
1 to 2 teaspoons hot pepper sauce
1 cup (4 ounces) shredded Cheddar cheese
1 cup (4 ounces) shredded Monterey Jack cheese

*Two cans (6 ounces each) fancy crabmeat, drained, can be substituted for fresh crabmeat.

1. Preheat broiler. Place muffin halves on lightly greased baking sheet. Broil 4 inches from heat 2 minutes or until muffins are lightly toasted. Place on large microwavable plate.

2. Melt butter in medium skillet over medium heat. Add green onions and bell pepper; cook and stir 3 to 4 minutes or until tender. Remove from heat; stir in crabmeat, hot pepper sauce and cheeses. Spoon about ⅓ cup crab mixture onto muffin halves.

3. Microwave at HIGH 2 to 3 minutes, rotating platter once, or until crab mixture is heated through.

Prep and cook time: 12 minutes

99¢ OR LESS Roasted Potato and Tuna Salad

Makes 4 servings

2 large baking potatoes, unpeeled
3 tablespoons vegetable oil
3 tablespoons orange juice
2 tablespoons lemon juice
2 tablespoons Dijon mustard
½ teaspoon salt
⅛ teaspoon coarsely ground black pepper
1 can (6 ounces) solid albacore tuna packed in water, drained and flaked
2 large tomatoes, seeded and coarsely chopped
¼ cup thinly sliced green onions
4 romaine lettuce leaves, washed

1. Preheat oven to 400°F. Spray jelly-roll pan with nonstick cooking spray.

2. Scrub potatoes; pat dry. Cut potatoes into ½-inch cubes. Place on prepared pan; coat potatoes with cooking spray. Arrange in single layer. Bake 20 to 25 minutes or until potatoes are tender and lightly browned, stirring occasionally.

3. While the potatoes are baking, combine oil, orange juice, lemon juice, mustard, salt and pepper in small bowl. Whisk until well blended.

4. Place potatoes in large bowl; cool slightly. Add tuna, tomatoes, green onions and oil mixture; toss gently to coat. Cover and chill at least 1 hour or up to 24 hours.

5. To complete recipe, let salad stand at room temperature 10 minutes. Toss gently and serve on lettuce leaves.

Make-ahead time: 1 hour or up to 24 hours before serving
Final prep time: 10 minutes

Roasted Potato and Tuna Salad

 **Easy Greek Salad**

Makes 6 servings

> 6 leaves romaine lettuce, washed and torn into 1½-inch pieces
> 1 cucumber, peeled and sliced
> 1 tomato, chopped
> ½ cup sliced red onion
> 1 ounce feta cheese, crumbled (about ⅓ cup)
> 2 tablespoons extra-virgin olive oil
> 2 tablespoons lemon juice
> 1 teaspoon dried oregano leaves
> ½ teaspoon salt

1. Combine lettuce, cucumber, tomato, onion and cheese in large serving bowl.

2. Whisk together oil, lemon juice, oregano and salt in small bowl. Pour over lettuce mixture; toss until coated. Serve immediately.

Prep time: 10 minutes

 **Curried Walnut Grain Burgers**

Makes 4 servings

> 2 eggs
> ⅓ cup plain yogurt
> 2 teaspoons Worcestershire sauce
> 2 teaspoons curry powder
> ½ teaspoon salt
> ¼ teaspoon ground red pepper
> 1⅓ cups cooked couscous or brown rice
> ½ cup finely chopped walnuts
> ½ cup grated carrot
> ½ cup minced green onions
> ⅓ cup fine, dry plain bread crumbs
> 4 sesame seed hamburger buns
>   Honey mustard
>   Thinly sliced cucumber or apple

1. Combine eggs, yogurt, Worcestershire sauce, curry, salt and red pepper in large bowl; beat until blended. Stir in couscous, walnuts, carrot, green onions and bread crumbs. Shape into 4 (1-inch-thick) patties.

2. Coat grill rack with nonstick cooking spray; place rack on grill over medium-hot coals (350° to 400°F). Grill burgers 5 to 6 minutes on each side or until done. Serve on buns with mustard and cucumber.

Prep and cook time: 25 minutes

Serving Suggestion: Serve with carrot sticks and alfalfa sprouts.

 **Hot Dogs with Dijon Kraut**

Makes 6 servings

> 1 (14-ounce) can sauerkraut
> ¼ cup GREY POUPON® Dijon Mustard
> ¼ cup prepared barbecue sauce
> ⅓ cup chopped onion
> 1 tablespoon sweet pickle relish
> 1 teaspoon caraway seed
> 6 hot dogs, grilled
> 6 oblong sandwich buns or hot dog rolls, toasted
> 1½ cups shredded Cheddar cheese (6 ounces)

In medium saucepan, over medium heat, heat sauerkraut, mustard, barbecue sauce, onion, pickle relish and caraway seed to a boil; reduce heat. Cover; simmer for 2 minutes. Keep warm.

Place hot dogs in buns; top each with ¼ cup cheese. Broil for 1 minute or until cheese melts. Top with sauerkraut mixture and serve immediately.

Curried Walnut Grain Burger

99¢ OR LESS Homemade Pizza

Makes 4 to 6 servings

½ tablespoon active dry yeast
1 teaspoon sugar, divided
½ cup warm water (105° to 115°F)
1¾ cups all-purpose flour, divided
¾ teaspoon salt, divided
2 tablespoons olive oil, divided
1 can (14½ ounces) whole peeled tomatoes, undrained
1 medium onion, chopped
1 clove garlic, minced
2 tablespoons tomato paste
1 teaspoon dried oregano leaves, crushed
½ teaspoon dried basil leaves, crushed
⅛ teaspoon ground black pepper
1¾ cups shredded mozzarella cheese
½ cup freshly grated Parmesan cheese
½ small red bell pepper, cored and seeded
½ small green bell pepper, cored and seeded
4 fresh medium mushrooms
1 can (2 ounces) flat anchovy fillets, drained (optional)
⅓ cup pitted ripe olives, halved

Sprinkle yeast and ½ teaspoon sugar over ½ cup warm water in small bowl; stir until yeast is dissolved. Let stand 5 minutes or until mixture is bubbly.

Place 1½ cups flour and ¼ teaspoon salt in medium bowl; stir in yeast mixture and 1 tablespoon oil, stirring until smooth, soft dough forms. Place dough on lightly floured surface; flatten slightly. Knead dough using as much of remaining flour as needed to form a stiff, elastic dough.

Shape dough into a ball; place in greased bowl. Turn to grease entire surface. Cover with clean kitchen towel and let dough rise in warm place 30 to 45 minutes or until doubled in bulk. Press two fingertips about ½ inch into dough. Dough is ready if indentations remain after fingers are removed.

For sauce, finely chop tomatoes in can with knife, reserving juice. Heat remaining 1 tablespoon oil in medium saucepan over medium heat. Add onion; cook 5 minutes or until soft. Add garlic; cook 30 seconds more. Add tomatoes and juice, tomato paste, oregano, basil, remaining ½ teaspoon sugar, ½ teaspoon salt and black pepper. Bring to a boil; reduce heat to medium-low. Simmer, uncovered, 10 to 15 minutes or until sauce thickens, stirring occasionally. Pour into bowl; cool.

Punch dough down. Knead briefly on lightly floured surface to distribute air bubbles; let dough rest 5 minutes more. Flatten dough into circle on lightly floured surface. Roll out dough, starting at center and rolling to edges, into 10-inch circle. Place circle in greased 12-inch pizza pan; stretch and pat dough out to edges of pan. Crimp edges to form rim. Cover and let stand 15 minutes.

Preheat oven to 450°F. Mix mozzarella and Parmesan cheeses in small bowl. Cut bell peppers into ¾-inch pieces. Trim mushroom stems; wipe clean with damp kitchen towel and thinly slice. Spread sauce evenly over pizza dough. Sprinkle with ⅔ of cheeses. Arrange bell peppers, mushrooms, anchovies, if desired, and olives over cheese. Sprinkle remaining cheeses on top. Bake 20 minutes or until crust is golden brown. To serve, cut into wedges.

Homemade Pizza

 ## Jicama and Black Bean Salad

Makes 4 servings

1½ pounds jicama, peeled and cut into short, thin
    strips (about 4 cups)
1 can (15 ounces) black beans, drained and rinsed
1 medium red bell pepper, finely chopped
½ cup chopped red onion
¼ cup packed fresh cilantro leaves, chopped
½ cup garlic-vinaigrette salad dressing
1 tablespoon lime juice
8 romaine lettuce leaves, washed and dried
⅔ cup (2½ ounces) shredded Cheddar cheese

1. Combine jicama, beans, bell pepper, onion and cilantro in large bowl.

2. Blend dressing and lime juice in small bowl; pour over jicama mixture. Toss well. Add salt and black pepper to taste.

3. Arrange 2 lettuce leaves on each plate. Spoon salad over lettuce; top with cheese.

Prep and cook time: 17 minutes

 ## Antipasto Salad Stack

Makes 6 main-dish servings

8 ounces uncooked rotini
2 medium tomatoes, halved lengthwise and thinly
    sliced
3 ounces sliced pepperoni, divided
1 can (15 ounces) red kidney beans or black beans,
    rinsed and drained
½ cup pimiento-stuffed green olives
¾ cup grated Parmesan cheese
1 bottle (8 ounces) Italian salad dressing
6 to 8 large romaine lettuce leaves, washed and
    thinly sliced

1. Cook pasta according to package directions; drain. Cool slightly.

2. While pasta is cooking, arrange tomatoes and half of pepperoni around bottom edge of 3-quart glass serving bowl.

3. Layer cooked pasta, remaining pepperoni, beans, olives and cheese in bowl; drizzle with salad dressing.

4. Top with lettuce; cover and chill at least 1 hour or up to 24 hours.

5. To complete recipe, toss salad gently just before serving.

Make-ahead time: at least 1 hour or up to 24 hours

Final prep time: 5 minutes

 ## Egg Salad Sandwiches

Makes 6 servings

1 cup EGG BEATERS® Healthy Real Egg Substitute,
    hard-cooked and chopped*
¼ cup chopped celery
¼ cup chopped onion
2 tablespoons fat-free mayonnaise
12 slices whole wheat bread, divided
6 lettuce leaves
1 large tomato, cut into 6 thin slices

*Hard-cooked: Pour ½ cup Egg Beaters into a nonstick skillet. Cover; cook for 10 minutes on very low heat. Cool, then chop into cubes.

In small bowl, combine hard-cooked Egg Beaters, celery, onion and mayonnaise. On each of 6 bread slices, place lettuce leaf and tomato slice; top each with about ¼ cup egg salad and remaining bread slice.

Final prep time: 20 minutes

Warm Couscous Salad

99¢ OR LESS Warm Couscous Salad

Makes 6 servings

2½ cups chicken broth
  2 cups uncooked couscous
  ¼ cup olive oil, divided
  1 onion, chopped
  1 green bell pepper, chopped
  1 teaspoon bottled minced garlic
  ¼ teaspoon salt
  ¼ teaspoon ground cumin
  ¼ teaspoon ground cinnamon
  ¼ teaspoon black pepper
  1 can (14½ ounces) Italian-style diced tomatoes, drained
  ¼ cup chopped walnuts

1. Bring chicken broth to a boil over high heat. Place couscous in serving bowl; pour broth over couscous and stir. Cover and let stand 10 minutes.

2. While couscous is cooking, heat 2 tablespoons oil in large nonstick skillet over medium heat. Add onion, bell pepper, garlic, salt, cumin, cinnamon and black pepper; cook and stir 2 minutes. Add tomatoes; cook 5 minutes.

3. Add tomato mixture and remaining 2 tablespoons oil to couscous; stir gently to combine.

4. Add walnuts to same skillet. Cook and stir over medium-high heat 2 minutes or until toasted. Sprinkle over salad before serving.

Prep and cook time: 25 minutes

99¢ OR LESS Mediterranean Microwave Meat Loaf

Makes 4 servings

1 pound lean ground beef
¼ pound Italian sausage
½ cup dry bread crumbs
¼ cup grated Parmesan cheese
1 large egg
⅓ cup plus 2 tablespoons prepared pasta sauce, divided
2 tablespoons lemon juice, divided
½ teaspoon ground allspice
¼ teaspoon black pepper

1. In large bowl, combine ground beef, sausage (if in links, remove casing), bread crumbs, cheese, egg, ⅓ cup pasta sauce, 1 tablespoon lemon juice, allspice and pepper. Mix until blended. Pat into ball. Place in 9-inch glass pie plate or shallow microwavable casserole 9 to 10 inches in diameter. Press into 7-inch circle.

2. Microwave, uncovered, on HIGH 8 minutes. Pour off drippings. Meanwhile, combine remaining 2 tablespoons pasta sauce and 1 tablespoon lemon juice; spread over top of meat loaf. Microwave 3 to 5 minutes more or until meat loaf registers 150°F in center. Let stand 5 minutes before serving.

Prep and cook time: 20 minutes

Serving Suggestion: Serve with frozen stuffed potatoes heated according to package directions and tossed green salad.

Mediterranean Microwave Meat Loaf

99¢ OR LESS Potato and Egg Pie

Makes 6 servings

1 (20-ounce) package frozen O'Brien hash brown potatoes, thawed
⅓ cup WESSON® Vegetable Oil
1½ tablespoons chopped fresh parsley, divided
¾ cup shredded pepper-jack cheese
¾ cup shredded Swiss cheese
1 (12-ounce) package bulk breakfast sausage, cooked, crumbled and drained
1 (4-ounce) can sliced mushrooms, drained
½ cup milk
4 eggs, beaten
1 teaspoon garlic salt
¼ teaspoon pepper
4 to 6 thin tomato slices

Preheat oven to 425°F. In a medium bowl, combine potatoes and Wesson Oil; blend to coat. Press mixture into a 10-inch pie dish. Bake for 30 minutes or until golden brown; remove from oven. Reduce oven temperature to 350°F. Meanwhile, in a large bowl, combine *1 tablespoon* parsley and *remaining* ingredients *except* tomato slices; blend well. Pour into potato crust. Bake for 25 minutes or until eggs are set. Place tomato slices over pie and top with *remaining* parsley. Bake 5 to 7 minutes longer.

Garden Tuna Salad

Makes 4 servings

  1 can (6 ounces) tuna packed in water, drained
  1 medium carrot, chopped
  1 rib celery, chopped
  ½ cup (2 ounces) reduced-fat Monterey Jack cheese
    cubes (¼ inch)
  ¼ cup frozen green peas, thawed and drained
  ¼ teaspoon dried parsley flakes
  ⅓ cup reduced-fat Italian salad dressing
  2 rounds pita bread, cut into halves
    Lettuce
    Tomato slices

1. Place tuna in large bowl; break into chunks.

2. Add carrot, celery, cheese, peas and parsley; toss to blend. Pour dressing over mixture; toss lightly to coat.

3. Place one piece lettuce and one tomato slice in each pita half. Fill with tuna salad.

Prep time: 15 minutes

Cheese and Bean Quesadillas

Makes 3 servings

  1 can (15 ounces) pinto beans, rinsed and drained
  ½ cup salsa
  1 teaspoon chili powder
  4 (10-inch) flour tortillas
  1 cup (4 ounces) shredded low-sodium, reduced-fat
    Monterey Jack cheese
  ¼ cup chopped fresh cilantro
  ¼ cup reduced-fat sour cream

1. Place beans in medium saucepan. Mash beans with potato masher or fork. Stir in salsa and chili powder. Cook and stir over medium heat until bubbly. Reduce heat to low. Simmer 5 minutes, adding more salsa if mixture becomes dry.

2. Spray griddle with nonstick cooking spray. Heat over medium heat until hot. Brush 1 tortilla lightly on both sides with water. Heat on griddle until lightly browned. Turn tortilla. Spread with half the bean mixture; sprinkle with ½ cup cheese and 2 tablespoons cilantro. Top with a second tortilla and press lightly. Brush top of tortilla with water. Carefully turn quesadilla to brown and crisp second side. Remove from heat; repeat with remaining tortillas. Cut each quesadilla into 6 wedges. Serve with sour cream. Garnish with fresh cilantro, if desired.

Ready to serve in 20 minutes.

Caesar Salad

Makes 8 servings

  12 cups torn romaine lettuce leaves
  ½ cup EGG BEATERS® Healthy Real Egg Substitute
  ¼ cup olive oil*
  ¼ cup lemon juice
  1 teaspoon Grey Poupon® Dijon mustard
  2 cloves garlic, minced
  ¼ teaspoon ground black pepper
    Grated Parmesan cheese, optional

*Vegetable oil can be substituted.

Place lettuce in large bowl; set aside.

In small bowl, whisk together Egg Beaters, oil, lemon juice, mustard, garlic and pepper until well blended. To serve, pour dressing over lettuce, tossing until well coated. Serve with Parmesan cheese, if desired.

Prep time: 15 minutes

Cheese and Bean Quesadillas

PENNY–PINCHING
Pasta, Beans & Rice

Explore the versatile world of pasta, beans and rice. Discover mouthwatering recipes bursting with a variety of flavor sensations that are sure to awaken your taste buds. From classic Fettuccine with Pesto to Beef & Bean Burritos exploding with robust flavor and topped with zesty salsa and rich sour cream, the perfect mealtime choice is just around the corner.

 Sweet and Sour Beef

Makes 4 servings

1 pound lean ground beef
1 small onion, thinly sliced
2 teaspoons minced fresh ginger
1 package (16 ounces) frozen mixed vegetables (snap peas, carrots, water chestnuts, pineapple and red pepper)
6 to 8 tablespoons bottled sweet and sour sauce or sauce from frozen mixed vegetables
Cooked rice

1. Place meat, onion and ginger in large skillet; cook over high heat 6 to 8 minutes or until no longer pink, breaking meat apart with wooden spoon. Pour off drippings.

2. Stir in frozen vegetables and sauce. Cook, covered, 6 to 8 minutes, stirring every 2 minutes or until vegetables are heated through. Serve over rice.

Prep and cook time: 15 minutes

Serving Suggestion: Serve with sliced Asian apple-pears.

Sweet and Sour Beef

Tuscany Cavatelli

Makes 5 (2-cup) servings

16 ounces uncooked cavatelli pasta, penne or ziti
1½ cups diced tomatoes, seeded
⅔ cup sliced pimiento-stuffed green olives
¼ cup capers, drained
2 tablespoons olive oil
2 tablespoons grated Parmesan cheese
2 tablespoons balsamic vinegar
½ teaspoon black pepper
2 cloves garlic, minced

1. Cook pasta according to package directions, omitting salt. Drain; set aside.

2. Combine tomatoes, olives, capers, oil, cheese, vinegar, pepper and garlic in a medium bowl. Stir in pasta until thoroughly coated. Serve warm or at room temperature. Garnish with fresh rosemary and basil leaves, if desired.

Prep time: 10 minutes
Cook time: 10 minutes

Straw and Hay Fettuccine

Makes 8 servings

6 ounces plain fettuccine, uncooked
6 ounces spinach fettuccine, uncooked
8 ounces fresh mushrooms, sliced
2 teaspoons margarine
2 cups fresh or frozen peas
4 tablespoons low-fat ricotta cheese
4 tablespoons skim milk
2 tablespoons grated Parmesan cheese

Prepare pasta according to package directions; drain. Sauté mushrooms in margarine in large skillet over low heat 5 minutes. Add peas. Cover; cook until tender. Remove from heat; set aside. In small bowl, combine ricotta cheese, milk and Parmesan cheese. Add cheese mixture to mushrooms and peas. Toss with pasta and serve.

Favorite recipe from **National Pasta Association**

Stuffed Shells Florentine

Makes 8 servings

1 cup (about 4 ounces) coarsely chopped mushrooms
½ cup chopped onion
1 clove garlic, minced
1 teaspoon Italian seasoning
¼ teaspoon ground black pepper
1 tablespoon FLEISCHMANN'S® 70% Corn Oil Spread
1 (16-ounce) container fat-free cottage cheese
1 (10-ounce) package frozen chopped spinach, thawed and well drained
½ cup EGG BEATERS® Healthy Real Egg Substitute
24 jumbo pasta shells, cooked in unsalted water and drained
1 (15¼-ounce) jar reduced-sodium spaghetti sauce, divided

In large skillet, over medium-high heat, sauté mushrooms, onion, garlic, Italian seasoning and pepper in spread until tender. Remove from heat; stir in cottage cheese, spinach and Egg Beaters. Spoon mixture into shells.

Spread ½ cup spaghetti sauce in bottom of 13×9×2-inch baking dish; arrange shells over sauce. Top with remaining sauce; cover. Bake at 350°F for 35 minutes or until hot.

Prep time: 30 minutes
Cook time: 40 minutes

Stuffed Shells Florentine

 **Tri-Color Pasta**

Makes 4 servings

> 1 package (16 ounces) tri-color pasta*
> 2 cups BIRDS EYE® frozen Green Peas
> 2 plum tomatoes, chopped or 1 red bell pepper, chopped
> 1 cup shredded mozzarella cheese
> ⅓ cup, or to taste, prepared pesto sauce

*Or, substitute 1 bag (16 ounces) frozen tortellini.

• In large saucepan, cook pasta according to package directions. Add peas during last 5 minutes; drain in colander. Rinse under cold water to cool.

• In large bowl, combine pasta, peas, tomatoes and cheese. Stir in pesto.

Prep time: 5 minutes
Cook time: 10 minutes

 **Spanish-Style Couscous**

Makes 4 servings

> 1 cup couscous
> 1 pound lean ground beef
> ½ medium onion, chopped
> 2 cloves garlic, minced
> 1 teaspoon ground cumin
> ½ teaspoon dried thyme leaves
> 1 can (about 14 ounces) beef broth
> ½ cup pimiento-stuffed green olives, sliced
> 1 small green bell pepper, seeded and cut into ½-inch pieces

1. Bring 1⅓ cups water to a boil over high heat in 1-quart saucepan. Stir in couscous. Cover; remove from heat.

2. Place beef in large skillet; cook over high heat 6 to 8 minutes or until no longer pink, breaking beef apart with wooden spoon. Pour off drippings. Add onion, garlic, cumin and thyme; cook and stir 30 seconds or until onion and garlic are tender. Add beef broth and olives; bring to a boil. Boil, uncovered, 5 minutes. Add pepper; cover and simmer 5 minutes more or until broth is reduced by half. Fluff couscous with fork. Spoon couscous onto plates or into serving bowls. Spoon beef mixture and broth over couscous.

Prep and cook time: 20 minutes

Serving Suggestion: Serve with carrot sticks.

 **Tarragon Tuna Pasta Salad**

Makes 4 servings

> ½ cup mayonnaise
> ½ teaspoon dried tarragon or thyme, crushed
> 3 cups chilled cooked mostaccioli or elbow macaroni
> 2 stalks celery, sliced
> 1 can (6⅛ ounces) solid white tuna in water, drained and broken into bite-sized pieces
> 1 can (14½ ounces) DEL MONTE® Peas and Carrots, drained

1. In large bowl, combine mayonnaise and tarragon. Add pasta, celery and tuna. Gently stir in peas and carrots.

2. Cover serving plates with lettuce, if desired. Top with salad. Garnish, if desired.

Prep Time: 8 minutes

Healthy Hint: Use light mayonnaise instead of regular mayonnaise.

Peanut Sauce over Vegetables and Pasta

99¢ OR LESS Peanut Sauce over Vegetables and Pasta

Makes 6 servings

1 package (16 ounces) frozen Oriental vegetable
    mixture (broccoli, red pepper and mushrooms)
⅔ cup skim milk
⅓ cup reduced-fat peanut butter
¼ cup reduced-sodium soy sauce
2 tablespoons fresh lime juice
½ teaspoon minced peeled fresh ginger
¼ teaspoon curry powder
¼ teaspoon red pepper flakes
6 cups cooked small pasta shells
3 green onions, thinly sliced

1. Cook frozen vegetables according to package directions; drain well. Set aside.

2. Combine milk and peanut butter in medium saucepan over medium heat, blending well with fork. Add soy sauce, lime juice, ginger, curry powder and red pepper flakes; stir to blend. Remove from heat and cool.

3. Add peanut sauce to vegetables. Spoon mixture over cooked pasta and top with green onions.

Prep and cook time: 20 minutes

Serving Suggestion: Serve with a fresh green salad or a cucumber and tomato medley.

Puerto Rican Sofrito Beans with Rice

99¢ OR LESS

Makes 4 to 5 servings

1 green bell pepper, cut into quarters
1 small onion, cut in half
½ cup chopped cilantro
3 tablespoons olive oil, divided
1 tablespoon bottled minced garlic
1½ teaspoons salt, divided
1 teaspoon ground cumin
¼ teaspoon ground red pepper
2 medium tomatoes, chopped
1 can (8 ounces) tomato sauce
1 can (15 ounces) black beans, rinsed and drained
1 can (15 ounces) red beans, rinsed and drained
1½ cups long-grain rice

1. Place bell pepper, onion and cilantro in food processor; process until finely chopped.

2. Heat 2 tablespoons oil in large skillet. Add bell pepper mixture, garlic, ½ teaspoon salt, cumin and ground red pepper; cook 5 minutes. Stir in tomatoes and tomato sauce; cook 5 minutes. Stir in beans; cook 5 minutes. At this point, bean mixture may be chilled up to 2 days.

3. To complete recipe, combine rice, 2¾ cups water, remaining 1 tablespoon oil and 1 teaspoon salt in medium saucepan. Bring to a boil over high heat. Reduce heat to low; cover and simmer 20 minutes or until water is absorbed.

4. While rice is cooking, heat bean mixture in large saucepan over low heat, stirring occasionally, until heated through (or microwave on HIGH 8 to 10 minutes, stirring after 5 minutes).

Make-ahead time: up to 2 days before serving
Final prep and cook time: 25 minutes

For a special touch, stir a handful of chopped cilantro and finely chopped red bell pepper into the rice just before serving.

Serving Suggestion: Press cooked rice into coffee or custard cups sprayed with nonstick cooking spray. Unmold onto individual plates or bowls; serve bean mixture around rice.

Fettuccine with Pesto

BUDGET MEAL

Makes 4 to 6 servings

12 ounces uncooked fettuccine
3 cups (1 ounce) loosely packed fresh basil leaves
⅔ cup grated Romano or Parmesan cheese
½ cup chopped California walnuts
½ cup olive oil
2 cloves garlic, peeled
¼ teaspoon salt
¼ teaspoon black pepper

Cook pasta according to package directions; drain. Meanwhile, place basil, cheese, walnuts, oil, garlic, salt and pepper in food processor or blender; process until well blended. (Sauce will thin out over hot pasta.) Place hot pasta in large bowl; add sauce. Toss until well coated. Serve immediately.

Favorite recipe from **Walnut Marketing Board**

Puerto Rican Sofrito Beans with Rice

 ## Lemon Chicken and Vegetables

Makes 8 (1-cup) servings

8 ounces uncooked spaghetti
1 pound boneless skinless chicken breasts
1 large green bell pepper, cut in half
1 large red bell pepper, cut in half
1 medium yellow squash, cut in half lengthwise
½ cup finely chopped fresh parsley
⅓ cup dry white wine
2 tablespoons fresh lemon juice
2 tablespoons olive oil
3 cloves garlic, minced
2 teaspoons finely grated lemon peel
¼ teaspoon salt
¼ teaspoon black pepper

1. Cook pasta according to package directions, omitting salt. Drain; set aside.

2. To prevent sticking, spray grid with nonstick cooking spray. Prepare coals for grilling. Place chicken, bell peppers and squash on grill 5 to 6 inches from medium-hot coals. Grill 10 to 12 minutes or until chicken is no longer pink in center and vegetables are soft to the touch. Remove from grill. Cool slightly; cut into ½-inch pieces.

3. Combine parsley, wine, lemon juice, oil, garlic, lemon peel, salt and black pepper in medium bowl. Toss cooked chicken and vegetables with ⅓ cup sauce. Toss pasta with remaining sauce. Place chicken and vegetables over pasta; serve.

Prep time: 15 minutes
Cook time: 15 minutes

 ## Pasta with Spinach and Ricotta

Makes 4 servings

8 ounces uncooked tri-colored rotini
1 box (10 ounces) frozen chopped spinach, thawed and drained
2 teaspoons bottled minced garlic
1 cup fat-free or part-skim ricotta cheese
3 tablespoons grated Parmesan cheese, divided

1. Cook pasta according to package directions; drain.

2. While pasta is cooking, coat large skillet with nonstick cooking spray; heat over medium-low heat. Add spinach and garlic; cook and stir 5 minutes. Stir in ricotta cheese, half of Parmesan cheese and ½ cup water; season with salt and pepper to taste.

3. Add pasta to skillet; stir until well blended. Sprinkle with remaining Parmesan cheese.

Prep and cook time: 24 minutes

Note: For extra flavor and color, add a chopped fresh tomato or a can of diced tomatoes to the skillet with the pasta.

For a special touch, garnish with fresh basil leaves.

Lemon Chicken and Vegetables

 **Rice and Bean Salad**

Makes 6 servings

1 can (about 14½ ounces) chicken broth
2 cups uncooked instant brown rice
1 tablespoon olive oil
1 medium onion, chopped
3 cloves garlic, minced
2 medium carrots, cut into 1-inch julienne strips
1 medium zucchini, halved lengthwise and sliced diagonally
1 can (15½ ounces) red beans, drained
1 can (14½ ounces) Italian-style stewed tomatoes
½ cup grated Parmesan cheese
½ cup Italian salad dressing
¼ cup fresh basil leaves, finely chopped

1. Bring chicken broth to a boil in medium saucepan over high heat; add rice and cover. Reduce heat and cook 10 minutes or until chicken broth is absorbed. Remove from heat; set aside.

2. Heat oil in large skillet over medium-high heat. Add onion and garlic; cook and stir 2 to 3 minutes or until onion is tender. Add carrots and zucchini; cook and stir 3 to 4 minutes or until vegetables are crisp-tender. Remove from heat. Add beans, tomatoes and prepared rice; stir to combine.

3. Place rice mixture in large bowl. Cover with plastic wrap and refrigerate overnight.

4. To complete recipe, add Parmesan cheese, salad dressing and basil to rice mixture; toss lightly. Season to taste with black pepper.

Make-ahead time: Up to 2 days before serving
Final prep time: 5 minutes

Serving Suggestion: Serve with flaky breadsticks or croissants and juicy chunks of watermelon.

For a special touch, garnish with tomato slices, carrot curls and a fresh basil sprig.

 **Linguine with Fresh Tomato Basil Sauce**

Makes 6 servings

1 cup chopped onion
3 cloves garlic, minced
¼ teaspoon ground black pepper
2 tablespoons FLEISCHMANN'S® 70% Corn Oil Spread
2 cups sliced fresh mushrooms
3 large tomatoes, peeled, seeded and chopped
1 tablespoon dried basil leaves, crushed *or* ¼ cup chopped fresh basil
1 teaspoon sugar
12 ounces uncooked linguine, cooked according to package directions, omitting salt, drained, kept warm

In large skillet, cook and stir onion, garlic and pepper in spread over medium-high heat until onion is tender, about 3 minutes. Add mushrooms; cook 5 minutes. Add tomatoes, basil and sugar; bring to a boil. Reduce heat to low; simmer, uncovered, 15 to 20 minutes. Serve over linguine.

Rice and Bean Salad

Beef & Bean Burritos

Makes 6 servings

Nonstick cooking spray
½ pound beef round steak, cut into ½-inch pieces
3 cloves garlic, minced
1 can (about 15 ounces) pinto beans, rinsed and drained
1 can (4 ounces) diced mild green chilies, drained
¼ cup finely chopped fresh cilantro
6 (6-inch) flour tortillas
½ cup (2 ounces) shredded reduced-fat Cheddar cheese

1. Spray nonstick skillet with cooking spray; heat over medium heat until hot. Add steak and garlic; cook and stir 5 minutes or until steak is cooked to desired doneness.

2. Stir beans, chilies and cilantro into skillet; cook and stir 5 minutes or until heated through.

3. Spoon steak mixture evenly down center of each tortilla; sprinkle cheese evenly over each tortilla. Fold bottom end of tortilla over filling; roll to enclose. Garnish with salsa and nonfat sour cream, if desired.

Beef & Bean Burrito

Peppercorn Pasta and Bean Salad

Makes 4 servings

> 8 ounces uncooked rotelle or radiatore pasta
> 1 bag (16 ounces) BIRDS EYE® frozen Farm Fresh Mixtures Broccoli, Red Peppers, Onions & Mushrooms
> 1 can (15 ounces) garbanzo beans (chick-peas), drained
> ½ cup creamy peppercorn ranch salad dressing

• In large saucepan, cook pasta according to package directions. Add vegetables during last 7 minutes; drain in colander. Rinse under cold water to cool.

• In large bowl, combine pasta, vegetables, beans and dressing. Cover and refrigerate until ready to serve.

Prep time: 5 minutes
Cook time: 10 to 12 minutes

Variation: Add 1 can (6 ounces) tuna or salmon, drained and flaked, or 6 ounces cooked shrimp or cubed cooked chicken to the pasta mixture.

Beef Stroganoff

Makes 6 servings

> 12 ounces wide egg noodles
> 1 can (10 ounces) condensed cream of mushroom soup
> 1 cup (8 ounces) sour cream
> 1 packet (1¼ ounces) dry onion soup mix
> 1¼ to 1½ pounds lean ground beef
> ½ (10-ounce) package frozen peas

1. Place 3 quarts water in 8-quart stock pot; bring to a boil over high heat. Stir in noodles; boil, uncovered, 6 minutes or until tender. Drain.

2. Meanwhile, place mushroom soup, sour cream and onion soup mix in medium bowl. Stir until blended; set aside. Place beef in large skillet; cook over high heat 6 to 8 minutes or until meat is no longer pink, breaking beef apart with wooden spoon. Pour off drippings. Reduce heat to low. Add soup mixture; stir over low heat until bubbly. Stir in peas; heat through. Serve over noodles.

Prep and cook time: 20 minutes

Herbed Veggie Cheese and Rice

Makes 4 servings

> 1 bag (16 ounces) BIRDS EYE® frozen Farm Fresh Mixtures Broccoli, Green Beans, Pearl Onions & Red Peppers
> 2 cups cooked white rice
> 2 tablespoons grated Parmesan cheese
> 1 teaspoon dried basil
> 1 teaspoon dill weed
> ½ cup reduced-fat shredded Cheddar cheese
> ½ cup reduced-fat shredded Monterey Jack cheese

• In large saucepan, cook vegetables according to package directions; drain and return to saucepan.

• Add rice, using fork to keep rice fluffy.

• Add Parmesan cheese, basil, dill, and salt and pepper to taste.

• Add Cheddar and Monterey Jack cheeses; toss together. Cook over medium heat until heated through.

Prep time: 6 minutes
Cook time: 12 to 15 minutes

 **Chicken Curry**

Makes 2 servings

½ cup uncooked white rice
1 small onion
2 boneless skinless chicken breast halves
1 tablespoon butter or margarine
1 clove garlic, minced
1 teaspoon curry powder
¼ teaspoon ground ginger
1 cup coarsely chopped apple, divided
3 tablespoons raisins
1 teaspoon chicken bouillon granules
¼ cup plain nonfat yogurt
2 teaspoons all-purpose flour

1. Cook rice according to package directions.

2. While rice is cooking, cut onion into thin slices. Cut chicken into ¾-inch cubes.

3. Heat butter, garlic, curry powder and ginger in medium skillet over medium heat. Add chicken; cook and stir 2 minutes. Add onion, ¾ cup chopped apple and raisins; cook and stir 3 minutes. Stir in chicken bouillon and ¼ cup water. Reduce heat to low; cover and cook 2 minutes.

4. Combine yogurt and flour in small bowl. Stir several tablespoons liquid from skillet into yogurt mixture. Stir yogurt mixture back into skillet. Cook and stir just until mixture starts to boil.

5. Serve chicken curry over rice; garnish with remaining ¼ cup chopped apple.

Prep and cook time: 28 minutes

For a special touch, sprinkle chicken with green onion slivers just before serving.

Chicken Curry

 **Baked Pasta and Cheese Supreme**

Makes 4 servings

8 ounces uncooked fusilli pasta
8 ounces bacon, diced
½ onion, chopped
2 cloves garlic, minced
2 teaspoons dried oregano leaves, divided
1 can (8 ounces) tomato sauce
1 teaspoon hot pepper sauce (optional)
1½ cups (6 ounces) shredded Cheddar or Colby cheese
½ cup fresh bread crumbs (from 1 slice of white bread)
1 tablespoon melted butter

1. Preheat oven to 400°F. Cook pasta according to package directions; drain.

2. While pasta is cooking, cook bacon in large ovenproof skillet over medium heat until crisp; drain.

3. Add onion, garlic and 1 teaspoon oregano to skillet; cook and stir about 3 minutes or until onion is tender. Stir in tomato sauce and hot pepper sauce. Add cooked pasta and cheese to skillet; stir to coat.

4. Combine bread crumbs, remaining 1 teaspoon oregano and melted butter; sprinkle over pasta mixture. Bake about 5 minutes or until hot and bubbly.

Prep and cook time: 25 minutes

For a special touch, garnish with yellow pear tomatoes and fresh basil leaves.

Turkey Vegetable Chili Mac

Makes 6 servings

Nonstick cooking spray
¾ pound ground turkey breast
½ cup chopped onion
2 cloves garlic, minced
1 can (about 15 ounces) black beans, rinsed and drained
1 can (14½ ounces) Mexican-style stewed tomatoes, undrained
1 can (14½ ounces) no-salt-added diced tomatoes, undrained
1 cup frozen whole kernel corn
1 teaspoon Mexican seasoning
½ cup uncooked elbow macaroni
⅓ cup reduced fat sour cream

1. Spray large nonstick saucepan or Dutch oven with cooking spray; heat over medium heat until hot. Add turkey, onion and garlic; cook 5 minutes or until turkey is no longer pink, stirring to crumble.

2. Stir beans, tomatoes with liquid, corn and Mexican seasoning into saucepan; bring to a boil over high heat. Cover; reduce heat to low. Simmer 15 minutes, stirring occasionally.

3. Meanwhile, cook pasta according to package directions, omitting salt. Rinse; drain. Stir into saucepan. Simmer, uncovered, 2 to 3 minutes or until heated through.

4. Top each serving with dollop of sour cream before serving. Garnish as desired.

Sweet & Sour Vegetable Couscous

Makes 4 servings

1 can (14½ ounces) vegetable broth
1 box (10 ounces) uncooked couscous
1 tablespoon vegetable oil
3 cups frozen Oriental vegetable mix
⅓ cup stir-fry sauce
2 tablespoons honey
2 tablespoons lemon juice
¼ cup sliced almonds

1. Pour vegetable broth into medium saucepan; bring to a boil. Stir in couscous and oil. Remove from heat; cover and let stand 5 minutes or until liquid is absorbed. Fluff couscous with fork; cover to keep warm.

2. While broth is heating, place vegetables in microwavable dish. Microwave according to package directions; drain.

3. Combine stir-fry sauce, honey and lemon juice in small bowl. Pour over cooked vegetables; microwave on HIGH 1 minute.

4. Spoon couscous onto serving plates. Top with vegetable mixture and sprinkle with almonds.

Prep and cook time: 20 minutes

Hint: For extra flavor and crunch, toast almonds. Place in small nonstick skillet; cook and stir over medium heat 2 minutes or until golden brown. (Watch carefully to prevent burning.)

For a special touch, garnish with carrot cut-outs and chives.

Turkey Vegetable Chili Mac

BUDGET–WISE
Skillet Dishes

Stir up some fun tonight! Skillet dishes are every cook's idea of a casual, effortless meal. These fuss-free one-dish meals are quick to fix and easy to clean up. Serve them alone or with a simple accompaniment of fresh fruit, raw vegetables or hot bread. You'll be in and out of the kitchen in a flash. Presto! Dinner is served!

 Cheeseburger Macaroni

Makes 4 servings

- 1 cup mostaccioli or elbow macaroni, uncooked
- 1 pound ground beef
- 1 medium onion, chopped
- 1 can (14½ ounces) DEL MONTE® Original or Italian Recipe Stewed Tomatoes
- ¼ cup DEL MONTE® Tomato Ketchup
- 1 cup (4 ounces) shredded Cheddar cheese

1. Cook pasta according to package directions; drain.

2. In large skillet, brown meat with onion; drain. Season with salt and pepper, if desired. Stir in tomatoes, ketchup and pasta; heat through.

3. Top with cheese. Garnish, if desired.

Prep time: 8 minutes
Cook time: 15 minutes

Cheeseburger Macaroni

 ## Chicken Fried Rice

Makes 6 servings

½ cup sliced green onions
¼ cup sliced celery
¼ cup chopped red bell pepper
1 clove garlic, crushed
½ teaspoon grated gingerroot
¼ teaspoon crushed red pepper flakes
2 teaspoons peanut oil
6 tablespoons EGG BEATERS® Healthy Real Egg
    Substitute
3 cups cooked regular long-grain rice, prepared in
    unsalted water
2 cups cooked diced chicken
2 tablespoons reduced-sodium soy sauce
1 teaspoon sugar

In large nonstick skillet, over high heat, sauté green onions, celery, bell pepper, garlic, ginger and crushed red pepper in oil until tender-crisp. Pour Egg Beaters into skillet; cook, stirring occasionally until mixture is set. Stir in rice, chicken, soy sauce and sugar; cook until heated through.

Prep time: 20 minutes
Cook time: 30 minutes

 ## Jiffy Chicken Supper

Makes 4 servings

1 bag (16 ounces) BIRDS EYE® frozen Pasta Secrets
    White Cheddar or Creamy Peppercorn
¼ cup water
1 can (6½ ounces) chicken, drained
¼ cup pitted ripe olives, sliced
1 cup (8 ounces) plain yogurt
2 tablespoons chopped fresh parsley

• In large skillet, place Pasta Secrets and water. Bring to boil over high heat. Reduce heat to medium; cover and simmer 7 to 9 minutes or until pasta is tender.

• Stir in chicken and olives; cook 5 minutes more.

• In small bowl, combine yogurt and parsley.

• Stir yogurt mixture into Pasta Secrets mixture; cover and cook over low heat 1 minute or until heated through.

Prep time: 5 minutes
Cook time: 15 to 18 minutes

 ## Southwest Skillet

Makes 4 servings

1 cup cubed, cooked chicken breast
1 bag (16 ounces) BIRDS EYE® frozen Pasta Secrets
    Zesty Garlic
1 cup chunky salsa
½ teaspoon chili powder
½ cup chopped green or red bell pepper

• In large skillet, combine all ingredients.

• Cook over medium heat 10 to 15 minutes or until heated through.

Prep time: 5 minutes
Cook time: 15 minutes

Cheesy Southwest Skillet: Stir in ½ cup shredded Cheddar cheese during last 5 minutes. Cook until cheese is melted.

Creamy Southwest Skillet: Remove skillet from heat. Stir in ¼ cup sour cream before serving.

Chicken Fried Rice

 **Tempting Tuna Parmesano**

Makes 2 to 3 servings

 2 large cloves garlic
 1 package (9 ounces) refrigerated fresh angel hair pasta
 ¼ cup butter or margarine
 1 cup whipping cream
 1 cup frozen peas
 ¼ teaspoon salt
 1 can (6½ ounces) white tuna in water, drained
 ¼ cup grated Parmesan cheese, plus additional cheese for serving

1. Fill large deep skillet ¾ full with very hot tap water. Cover and bring to a boil over high heat. Meanwhile, peel and mince garlic.

2. Add pasta to skillet; boil 1 to 2 minutes or until pasta is firm to the bite. *(Do not overcook.)* Drain; set aside.

3. Add butter and garlic to skillet; cook over medium-high heat until butter is melted and sizzling. Stir in cream, peas and salt; bring to a boil.

4. Break tuna into chunks and stir into skillet with ¼ cup cheese. Return pasta to skillet; cook until heated through, tossing gently with 2 wooden spoons. Serve with additional cheese and pepper to taste.

Prep and cook time: 16 minutes

Serving Suggestion: Serve with a tossed romaine and tomato salad with Italian dressing.

 **Joe's Special**

Makes 6 servings

 1 pound lean ground beef
 1 small onion, chopped
 2 cups sliced mushrooms
 2 teaspoons Worcestershire sauce
 1 teaspoon dried oregano leaves
 1 teaspoon ground nutmeg
 ½ teaspoon garlic powder
 ½ teaspoon salt
 1 package (10 ounces) frozen chopped spinach, thawed
 4 large eggs, lightly beaten
 ⅓ cup grated Parmesan cheese

1. Spray large skillet with nonstick cooking spray. Combine beef, onion and mushrooms; cook over medium-high heat 6 to 8 minutes or until onion is tender, breaking beef apart with wooden spoon. Add Worcestershire, oregano, nutmeg, garlic powder and salt. Cook until beef is no longer pink.

2. Drain spinach (do not squeeze dry); stir into beef mixture. Push mixture to one side of pan. Reduce heat to medium. Pour eggs into other side of pan; cook, without stirring, 1 to 2 minutes or until set on bottom. Lift eggs to allow uncooked portion to flow underneath. Repeat until softly set. Gently stir into beef mixture and heat through. Stir in cheese.

Prep and cook time: 20 minutes

Serving Suggestion: Serve with salsa and toast.

Ham & Barbecued Bean Skillet

Ham & Barbecued Bean Skillet

Makes 4 servings

1 tablespoon vegetable oil
1 cup chopped onion (from the salad bar or frozen)
1 teaspoon bottled minced garlic
1 can (15 ounces) red or pink kidney beans, rinsed and drained
1 can (15 ounces) cannellini or Great Northern beans, rinsed and drained
1 cup chopped green bell pepper
½ cup firmly packed light brown sugar
½ cup catsup
2 tablespoons cider vinegar
2 teaspoons dry mustard
1 fully cooked smoked ham steak (about 12 ounces), cut ½ inch thick

1. Heat oil in large deep skillet over medium-high heat until hot. Add onion and garlic; cook 3 minutes, stirring occasionally.

2. Add kidney beans, cannellini beans, bell pepper, brown sugar, catsup, vinegar and mustard; mix well.

3. Trim fat from ham; cut into ½-inch pieces. Add ham to bean mixture; simmer over medium heat 5 minutes or until sauce thickens and mixture is heated through, stirring occasionally.

Prep and cook time: 20 minutes

Serving Suggestion: Serve with a Caesar salad and crisp breadsticks.

Thai-Style Warm Noodle Salad

Makes 4 servings

8 ounces uncooked spaghetti or angel hair pasta
½ cup chunky peanut butter
¼ cup soy sauce
¼ to ½ teaspoon red pepper flakes
2 green onions, thinly sliced
1 carrot, shredded

1. Cook pasta according to package directions.

2. While pasta is cooking, blend peanut butter, soy sauce and red pepper flakes in medium bowl until smooth.

3. Drain pasta, reserving 5 tablespoons water. Mix hot pasta water with peanut butter mixture until smooth; toss pasta with sauce. Stir in green onions and carrot. Serve warm or at room temperature.

Prep and cook time: 12 minutes

Beefy Bean & Walnut Stir-Fry

Makes 4 servings

1 teaspoon vegetable oil
3 cloves garlic, minced
1 pound lean ground beef or ground turkey
1 bag (16 ounces) BIRDS EYE® frozen Cut Green Beans, thawed
1 teaspoon salt
½ cup California walnut pieces

• In large skillet, heat oil and garlic over medium heat about 30 seconds.

• Add beef and beans; sprinkle with salt. Mix well.

• Cook 5 minutes or until beef is well browned, stirring occasionally.

• Stir in California walnuts; cook 2 minutes more.

Prep time: 5 minutes
Cook time: 7 to 10 minutes

Serving Suggestion: Serve over hot cooked egg noodles or rice.

Quick Skillet Rice Gratin

Makes 4 to 6 servings

2 tablespoons olive oil
1 onion, chopped
2 cloves garlic, minced
2 medium carrots, peeled and chopped
1 teaspoon dried thyme leaves
2 cups uncooked instant white rice
1 can (15½ ounces) kidney beans, rinsed and drained
1 teaspoon salt
⅓ cup grated Parmesan cheese

1. Heat oil in large skillet over medium-high heat until hot. Add onion and garlic; cook and stir 2 minutes. Add carrots and thyme; cook and stir 4 minutes more.

2. Add rice, 2 cups water, beans and salt; season to taste with black pepper. Stir well. Bring to a boil. Reduce heat to low. Sprinkle with cheese. Cover and simmer 5 minutes or until cheese is melted and all liquid is evaporated.

Prep and cook time: 15 minutes

Thai-Style Warm Noodle Salad

 **Bacon & Potato Frittata**

Makes 4 servings

> 2 cups frozen O'Brien-style potatoes with onions and peppers
> 3 tablespoons butter or margarine
> 5 eggs
> ½ cup canned real bacon pieces
> ¼ cup half-and-half or milk
> ⅛ teaspoon salt
> ⅛ teaspoon pepper

1. Preheat broiler. Place potatoes in a microwavable medium bowl; microwave on HIGH 1 minute.

2. Melt butter in large ovenproof skillet over medium-high heat. Swirl butter up side of pan to prevent eggs from sticking. Add potatoes; cook 3 minutes, stirring occasionally.

3. Beat eggs in medium bowl. Add bacon, half-and-half, salt and pepper; mix well.

4. Pour egg mixture into skillet; reduce heat to medium. Stir gently to incorporate potatoes. Cover and cook 6 minutes or until eggs are set at edges (top will still be wet).

5. Transfer skillet to broiler. Broil 4 inches from heat about 1 to 2 minutes or until center is set and frittata is golden brown. Cut into wedges.

Prep and cook time: 20 minutes

Serving Suggestion: Garnish frittata with red bell pepper strips, chopped chives and salsa.

 **Tuscan Pasta and Beans**

Makes 4 servings

> 1 package (8 ounces) pasta
> 2 to 3 teaspoons minced garlic
> 1 tablespoon vegetable oil
> 1 can (14¾ ounces) chicken broth
> 1 box (10 ounces) BIRDS EYE® frozen Chopped Spinach
> 1 can (15 ounces) white beans, drained
> Crushed red pepper flakes
> Grated Parmesan cheese

• In large saucepan, cook pasta according to package directions; drain.

• In large skillet, sauté garlic in oil over medium-high heat until garlic is tender. Add broth and spinach; cook according to spinach package directions.

• Stir in beans and pasta. Cook, uncovered, over medium-high heat until heated through.

• Season with pepper flakes and cheese to taste.

Prep time: 5 minutes
Cook time: 20 minutes

Variation: Add ½ pound Italian sausage, casings removed and sliced, with the garlic. Cook until sausage is browned. Continue as directed.

Serving Suggestion: Offer crusty Italian bread to soak up this flavorful broth.

Bacon & Potato Frittata

Vegetarian Stir-Fry

 Vegetarian Stir-Fry

Makes 4 servings

1 bag (16 ounces) BIRDS EYE® frozen Mixed
    Vegetables
2 tablespoons water
1 can (14 ounces) kidney beans, drained
1 jar (14 ounces) spaghetti sauce
½ teaspoon garlic powder
½ cup grated Parmesan cheese

• In large skillet, place vegetables in water. Cover; cook 7 to 10 minutes over medium heat.

• Uncover; stir in beans, spaghetti sauce and garlic powder; cook until heated through.

• Sprinkle with cheese.

Prep time: 2 minutes
Cook time: 12 to 15 minutes

Serving Suggestion: Serve over hot cooked rice or pasta.

 **Spicy Crabmeat Frittata**

Makes 4 servings

1 tablespoon olive oil
1 medium green bell pepper, finely chopped
2 cloves garlic, minced
6 eggs
1 can (6½ ounces) lump white crabmeat, drained
¼ teaspoon ground black pepper
¼ teaspoon salt
¼ teaspoon hot pepper sauce
1 large ripe plum tomato, seeded and finely chopped

1. Preheat broiler. Heat oil in 10-inch nonstick skillet with oven-safe handle over medium-high heat. Add bell pepper and garlic to skillet; cook 3 minutes or until softened.

2. While bell pepper and garlic cook, beat eggs in medium bowl. Add crabmeat; mix to break large pieces. Add ground pepper, salt and pepper sauce; blend well. Set aside.

3. Add tomato to skillet; cook and stir 1 minute. Add egg mixture to skillet. Reduce heat to medium-low; cook about 7 minutes or until eggs begin to set around edges.

4. Remove pan from burner and place under broiler 6 inches from heat. Broil about 2 minutes or until top of frittata is browned. Remove pan from broiler; slide frittata onto serving plate. Serve immediately.

Prep and cook time: 20 minutes

Serving Suggestion: Serve with crusty bread, cut-up fresh vegetables and chunky guacamole.

 **Fried Rice with Ham**

Makes 4 servings

2 tablespoons vegetable oil, divided
2 eggs, beaten
1 small onion, chopped
1 carrot, peeled and chopped
⅔ cup diced ham
½ cup frozen green peas
1 large clove garlic, minced
3 cups cold cooked rice
3 tablespoons reduced-sodium soy sauce
⅛ teaspoon pepper

1. Heat 1 tablespoon oil in wok or large skillet over medium-high heat until hot. Add eggs; rotate wok to swirl eggs into thin layer. Cook eggs until set and slightly brown; break up with wooden spoon. Remove from wok to small bowl.

2. Heat remaining 1 tablespoon oil until hot. Add onion and carrot; stir-fry 2 minutes. Add ham, peas and garlic; stir-fry 1 minute.

3. Add rice; cook and stir 2 to 3 minutes or until rice is heated through. Stir in soy sauce and pepper until well blended. Stir in cooked eggs.

Prep and cook time: 18 minutes

 ## Corn Bread Stuffing with Sausage and Apple

Makes 4 servings

⅓ cup pecan pieces
1 pound bulk pork sausage
1 large Jonathan apple
1⅓ cups chicken broth
¼ cup apple juice
6 ounces seasoned cornbread stuffing mix

1. Preheat oven to 300°F. Place nuts in shallow baking pan. Bake 6 to 8 minutes or until lightly browned, stirring frequently. Place sausage in large skillet; cook over high heat 10 minutes or until meat is no longer pink, breaking meat apart with wooden spoon. Pour off drippings.

2. While browning sausage, coarsely chop apple. Place in 3-quart saucepan. Add chicken broth, apple juice and seasoning packet. Bring to a boil, uncovered, over high heat. Remove from heat; stir in stuffing mix. Cover; let stand 3 to 5 minutes or until stuffing is moist and tender. Stir sausage into stuffing. Spoon into serving bowl and top with nuts.

Prep and cook time: 19 minutes

 ## Tofu Stir-Fry

Makes 4 servings

2 cups uncooked instant white rice
2 teaspoons vegetable oil
2 cups broccoli florets
1 large carrot, sliced
½ green bell pepper, sliced
¼ cup frozen chopped onion
½ cup teriyaki sauce
½ cup orange juice
1 tablespoon cornstarch
1 teaspoon bottled minced garlic
½ teaspoon ground ginger
¼ to ½ teaspoon hot pepper sauce
1 package (10½ ounces) reduced-fat firm tofu, drained and cubed

1. Cook rice according to package directions.

2. While rice is cooking, heat oil in large skillet. Add broccoli, carrot, bell pepper and onion; cook and stir 3 minutes.

3. Combine teriyaki sauce, orange juice, cornstarch, garlic, ginger and hot pepper sauce in small bowl; mix well. Pour sauce over vegetables in skillet. Bring to a boil; cook and stir 1 minute.

4. Add tofu to skillet; stir gently to coat with sauce. Serve over rice.

Prep and cook time: 18 minutes

Corn Bread Stuffing with Sausage and Apple

 **Bratwurst Skillet Breakfast**

Makes 4 servings

1½ pounds red potatoes
3 bratwurst links (about ¾ pound)
2 tablespoons butter or margarine
1½ teaspoons caraway seeds
4 cups shredded red cabbage

1. Cut potatoes into ¼- to ½-inch pieces. Place in microwavable casserole. Microwave, covered, on HIGH 3 minutes; stir. Microwave 2 minutes more or until just tender; set aside.

2. While potatoes are cooking, slice bratwurst into ¼-inch pieces. Place bratwurst in large skillet; cook over medium-high heat, stirring occasionally, 8 minutes or until browned and no longer pink in center. Remove bratwurst from pan with slotted spoon; set aside. Pour off drippings.

3. Melt butter in skillet. Add potatoes and caraway. Cook, stirring occasionally, 6 to 8 minutes or until potatoes are golden and tender. Return bratwurst to skillet; stir in cabbage. Cook, covered, 3 minutes or until cabbage is slightly wilted. Uncover and stir 3 to 4 minutes more or until cabbage is just tender yet still bright red.

Prep and cook time: 30 minutes

Serving Suggestion: Serve with fresh fruit and English muffin.

 **Noodles Thai Style**

Makes 6 (1-cup) servings

¼ cup ketchup
2 tablespoons reduced-sodium soy sauce
1 tablespoon sugar
¼ to ½ teaspoon crushed red pepper
¼ teaspoon ground ginger
2 teaspoons FLEISCHMANN'S® 70% Corn Oil Spread, divided
1 cup EGG BEATERS® Healthy Real Egg Substitute
8 green onions, cut in 1½-inch pieces
1 clove garlic, minced
¾ pound fresh bean sprouts, rinsed and well drained
8 ounces linguine, cooked and drained
¼ cup dry roasted unsalted peanuts, chopped

In small bowl, combine ketchup, soy sauce, sugar, pepper and ginger; set aside.

In large nonstick skillet, over medium heat, melt 1 teaspoon spread. Pour Egg Beaters into skillet. Cook, stirring occasionally until set. Remove to another small bowl.

In same skillet, over medium heat, sauté green onions and garlic in remaining spread for 2 minutes. Stir in bean sprouts; cook for 2 minutes. Stir in ketchup mixture. Cook until heated through. Transfer to large bowl; add eggs and linguine. Toss until combined. Top with peanuts.

Prep time: 25 minutes
Cook time: 5 minutes

Bratwurst Skillet Breakfast

COST-CUTTING
Casseroles

With these one-dish creations, preparing dinner will be a snap. Choose from hearty classics like Country-Style Lasagna and Creamy Beef and Vegetable Casserole or enticing contemporary fare such as Lemony Dill Salmon and Shell Casserole and Zucchini Mushroom Frittata. Whether it's a casual family gathering or a special dinner, you'll find the ideal homespun casserole to serve with style.

99¢ OR LESS Vegetable Strata

Makes 6 servings

2 slices white bread, cubed
¼ cup shredded reduced-fat Swiss cheese
½ cup sliced carrots
½ cup sliced mushrooms
¼ cup chopped onion
1 clove garlic, crushed
1 teaspoon FLEISCHMANN'S® 70% Corn Oil Spread
½ cup chopped tomato
½ cup snow peas
1 cup EGG BEATERS® Healthy Real Egg Substitute
¾ cup skim milk

Place bread cubes evenly into bottom of greased 1½-quart casserole dish. Sprinkle with cheese; set aside.

In medium nonstick skillet, over medium heat, sauté carrots, mushrooms, onion and garlic in spread until tender. Stir in tomato and snow peas; cook 1 to 2 minutes more. Spoon over cheese. In small bowl, combine Egg Beaters and milk; pour over vegetable mixture. Bake at 375°F for 45 to 50 minutes or until knife inserted in center comes out clean. Let stand 10 minutes before serving.

Prep time: 15 minutes
Cook time: 55 minutes

Vegetable Strata

Barbecue Chicken with Cornbread Topper

Makes 8 servings

1½ pounds boneless skinless chicken breasts and thighs
1 can (15 ounces) red beans, rinsed and drained
1 can (8 ounces) tomato sauce
1 cup chopped green bell pepper
½ cup barbecue sauce
1 envelope (6.5 ounces) cornbread mix
Ingredients for cornbread mix

1. Cut chicken into ¾-inch cubes. Heat nonstick skillet over medium heat. Add chicken; cook and stir 5 minutes or until cooked through.

2. Combine chicken, beans, tomato sauce, bell pepper and barbecue sauce in 8-inch microwavable ovenproof dish. Cover and refrigerate up to 2 days.

3. To complete recipe, preheat oven to 375°F. Loosely cover chicken mixture with plastic wrap or waxed paper. Microwave on MEDIUM-HIGH (70% power) 8 minutes or until heated through, stirring after 4 minutes.

4. While chicken mixture is heating, prepare cornbread mix according to package directions. Spoon batter over chicken mixture. Bake 15 to 18 minutes or until toothpick inserted in center of cornbread layer comes out clean.

Make-ahead time: up to 2 days before serving
Final prep and cook time: 28 minutes

Zucchini Mushroom Frittata

Makes 6 servings

1½ cups EGG BEATERS® Healthy Real Egg Substitute
½ cup (2 ounces) shredded reduced-fat Swiss cheese
¼ cup skim milk
½ teaspoon garlic powder
¼ teaspoon seasoned pepper
    Nonstick cooking spray
1 medium zucchini, shredded (1 cup)
1 medium tomato, chopped
1 (4-ounce) can sliced mushrooms, drained
    Tomato slices and fresh basil leaves, for garnish

In medium bowl, combine Egg Beaters, cheese, milk, garlic powder and seasoned pepper; set aside.

Spray 10-inch ovenproof nonstick skillet lightly with nonstick cooking spray. Over medium-high heat, sauté zucchini, tomato and mushrooms in skillet until tender. Pour egg mixture into skillet, stirring well. Cover; cook over low heat for 15 minutes or until cooked on bottom and almost set on top. Remove lid and place skillet under broiler for 2 to 3 minutes or until desired doneness. Slide onto serving platter; cut into wedges to serve. Garnish with tomato slices and basil.

Prep time: 20 minutes
Cook time: 20 minutes

Barbecue Chicken with Cornbread Topper

Asparagus Frittata Casserole

Makes 4 servings

3 large eggs
1½ cups 1% milk
1 teaspoon salt
1 box (10 ounces) BIRDS EYE® frozen Deluxe
    Asparagus Spears, thawed
½ cup shredded Monterey Jack or Cheddar cheese

• Preheat oven to 400°F.

• In medium bowl, beat eggs. Add milk and salt; blend well.

• Pour mixture into greased 9×9-inch baking pan; top with asparagus.

• Sprinkle with cheese.

• Bake 15 minutes or until egg mixture is set.

Prep time: 5 to 7 minutes
Cook time: 15 minutes

Mexican Strata Olé

Makes 8 servings

4 (6-inch) corn tortillas, halved, divided
1 cup chopped onion
½ cup chopped green bell pepper
1 clove garlic, crushed
1 teaspoon dried oregano leaves
½ teaspoon ground cumin
1 teaspoon FLEISCHMANN'S® 70% Corn Oil Spread
1 cup dried kidney beans, cooked in unsalted water
    according to package directions
½ cup (2 ounces) shredded reduced-fat Cheddar
    cheese
1½ cups skim milk
1 cup EGG BEATERS® Healthy Real Egg Substitute
1 cup thick and chunky salsa

Arrange half the tortilla pieces in bottom of greased 12×8×2-inch baking dish; set aside.

In large nonstick skillet, over medium-high heat, sauté onion, bell pepper, garlic, oregano and cumin in spread until tender; stir in beans. Spoon half the mixture over tortillas; repeat layers once. Sprinkle with cheese.

In medium bowl, combine milk and Egg Beaters; pour evenly over cheese. Bake at 350°F for 40 minutes or until puffed and golden brown. Let stand 10 minutes before serving. Serve topped with salsa.

Prep time: 25 minutes
Cook time: 50 minutes

Baked Cheesey Rotini

Makes 6 servings

¾ pound lean ground beef
½ cup chopped onion
2 cups cooked rotini, drained
1 (15-ounce) can HUNT'S® Ready Tomato Sauces
    Chunky Italian
¼ cup chopped green bell pepper
¾ teaspoon garlic salt
¼ teaspoon black pepper
1½ cups cubed processed American cheese

Preheat oven to 350°F. In large skillet, brown beef with onion; drain. Stir in rotini, tomato sauce, bell pepper, garlic salt and black pepper. Pour beef mixture into 1½-quart casserole. Top with cheese. Bake, covered, 20 minutes or until sauce is bubbly.

BUDGET MEAL Macaroni and Cheese Dijon

Makes 6 servings

1¼ cups milk

12 ounces pasteurized process Cheddar cheese spread, cubed

½ cup GREY POUPON® Dijon Mustard

⅓ cup sliced green onions

6 slices bacon, cooked and crumbled

⅛ teaspoon ground red pepper

12 ounces tri-color rotelle or spiral-shaped pasta, cooked

1 (2.8-ounce) can French fried onion rings

In medium saucepan, over low heat, heat milk, cheese and mustard until cheese melts and mixture is smooth. Stir in green onions, bacon and pepper; remove from heat.

In large bowl, combine hot pasta and cheese mixture, tossing until well coated; spoon into greased 2-quart casserole. Cover; bake at 350°F for 15 to 20 minutes. Uncover and stir; top with onion rings. Bake, uncovered, for 5 minutes more. Let stand 10 minutes before serving. Garnish as desired.

Macaroni and Cheese Dijon

99¢ OR LESS Lemony Dill Salmon and Shell Casserole

Makes 6 servings

6 ounces uncooked medium shell pasta
Nonstick cooking spray
1½ cups sliced mushrooms
⅓ cup sliced green onions
1 clove garlic, minced
2 cups skim milk
3 tablespoons all-purpose flour
1 tablespoon grated lemon peel
¾ teaspoon dried dill weed
¼ teaspoon salt
⅛ teaspoon ground black pepper
1½ cups frozen green peas
1 can (7½ ounces) salmon, drained and flaked

1. Preheat oven to 350°F. Cook pasta according to package directions, omitting salt. Rinse; drain. Set aside.

2. Spray medium nonstick saucepan with cooking spray; heat over medium heat until hot. Add mushrooms, onions and garlic; cook and stir 5 minutes or until vegetables are tender.

3. Combine milk and flour in medium bowl until smooth. Stir in lemon peel, dill weed, salt and pepper. Stir into saucepan; heat over medium-high heat 5 to 8 minutes or until thickened, stirring constantly. Remove saucepan from heat. Stir in pasta, peas and salmon. Pour pasta mixture into 2-quart casserole.

4. Bake, covered, 35 to 40 minutes. Serve immediately. Garnish as desired.

Lemony Dill Salmon and Shell Casserole

99¢ OR LESS Broccoli Lasagna Bianca

Makes 8 servings

1 (15- to 16-ounce) container fat-free ricotta cheese
1 cup EGG BEATERS® Healthy Real Egg Substitute
1 tablespoon minced basil (*or* 1 teaspoon dried basil leaves)
½ cup chopped onion
1 clove garlic, minced
2 tablespoons FLEISCHMANN'S® 70% Corn Oil Spread
¼ cup all-purpose flour
2 cups skim milk
2 (10-ounce) packages frozen chopped broccoli, thawed and well drained
1 cup (4 ounces) shredded part-skim mozzarella cheese
9 lasagna noodles, cooked and drained
1 small tomato, chopped
2 tablespoons grated Parmesan cheese
Fresh basil leaves, for garnish

In medium bowl, combine ricotta cheese, Egg Beaters and minced basil; set aside.

In large saucepan, over medium heat, sauté onion and garlic in spread until tender-crisp. Stir in flour; cook for 1 minute. Gradually stir in milk; cook, stirring until mixture thickens and begins to boil. Remove from heat; stir in broccoli and mozzarella cheese.

In lightly greased 13×9×2-inch baking dish, place 3 lasagna noodles; top with ⅓ each ricotta and broccoli mixtures. Repeat layers 2 more times. Top with tomato; sprinkle with Parmesan cheese. Bake at 350°F for 1 hour or until set. Let stand 10 minutes before serving. Garnish with basil leaves.

Prep time: 20 minutes
Cook time: 90 minutes

Country-Style Lasagna

99¢ OR LESS Country-Style Lasagna

Makes 6 servings

9 lasagna noodles (2 inches wide)
2 cans (14½ ounces each) DEL MONTE® Italian
    Recipe Stewed Tomatoes
  Milk
2 tablespoons butter or margarine
3 tablespoons all-purpose flour
1 teaspoon dried basil, crushed
1 cup diced cooked ham
2 cups (8 ounces) shredded mozzarella cheese

1. Cook noodles according to package directions; rinse, drain and separate noodles.

2. Meanwhile, drain tomatoes, reserving liquid; pour liquid into measuring cup. Add milk to measure 2 cups.

3. In large saucepan, melt butter; stir in flour and basil. Cook over medium heat 3 minutes, stirring constantly. Stir in reserved liquid; cook until thickened, stirring constantly. Season to taste with salt and pepper, if desired. Stir in tomatoes.

4. Spread thin layer of sauce on bottom of 11×7-inch or 2-quart baking dish. Top with 3 noodles and ⅓ *each* of sauce, ham and cheese; repeat layers twice, ending with cheese.

5. Bake uncovered at 375°F, 25 minutes. Serve with grated Parmesan cheese and garnish, if desired.

Prep time: 15 minutes
Cook time: 25 minutes

 **Creamy Beef and Vegetable Casserole**

Makes 4 servings

1 pound lean ground beef
1 small onion, chopped
1 can (16 ounces) BIRDS EYE® frozen Farm Fresh Mixtures Broccoli, Corn & Red Peppers
1 can (10¾ ounces) cream of mushroom soup

• In medium skillet, brown beef and onion; drain excess fat.

• Meanwhile, in large saucepan, cook vegetables according to package directions; drain.

• Stir in beef mixture and soup. Cook over medium heat until heated through.

Prep time: 5 minutes
Cook time: 10 to 15 minutes

Serving Suggestion: Serve over rice and sprinkle with ½ cup shredded Cheddar cheese.

 **Hamburger Casserole Olé**

Makes 4 servings

1 pound lean ground beef or ground turkey
1 package (1¼ ounces) taco seasoning mix
1 cup water
1 box (9 ounces) BIRDS EYE® frozen Cut Green Beans
½ cup shredded sharp Cheddar cheese
½ cup shredded mozzarella cheese

• Preheat oven to 325°F.

• Brown beef; drain excess fat. Add taco mix and water; cook over low heat 8 to 10 minutes or until liquid has been absorbed.

• Meanwhile, cook green beans according to package directions; drain.

• Spread meat in greased 13×9-inch baking pan. Spread beans over meat. Sprinkle with cheeses.

• Bake 15 to 20 minutes or until hot and cheese is melted.

Prep time: 15 minutes
Cook time: 20 minutes

Serving Suggestion: Serve over tortillas or corn chips and top with sour cream, chopped avocado, chopped lettuce and/or chopped tomatoes.

 **Spinach & Egg Casserole**

Makes 4 servings

1 box (10 ounces) BIRDS EYE® frozen Chopped Spinach
1 can (15 ounces) Cheddar cheese soup
1 tablespoon mustard
½ pound deli ham, cut into ¼-inch cubes
4 hard-boiled eggs, chopped or sliced

• Preheat oven to 350°F.

• In large saucepan, cook spinach according to package directions; drain well.

• Stir in soup, mustard and ham.

• Pour into 9×9-inch baking pan. Top with eggs.

• Bake 15 to 20 minutes or until heated through.

Prep time: 10 minutes
Cook time: 15 to 20 minutes

Serving Suggestion: Sprinkle with paprika for added color.

 **Easy Polenta Marinara**

Makes 6 servings

> 1 can (about 14 ounces) fat-free reduced sodium chicken broth
> 1 cup yellow cornmeal
> 3 tablespoons grated Parmesan cheese
> 1½ cups prepared marinara sauce
> ½ cup (2 ounces) shredded part-skim mozzarella cheese

1. Preheat oven to 375°F. Grease 9-inch square baking dish; set aside.

2. Combine broth and 1 cup water in medium saucepan. Whisk cornmeal into liquid. Bring to a boil over medium-high heat, stirring to prevent lumps.

3. Reduce heat to medium-low; cook about 7 minutes or until mixture is very thick, stirring constantly. Stir in Parmesan cheese; season with salt and pepper to taste.

4. Pour hot polenta into prepared dish, spreading evenly with spatula. Pour marinara sauce over polenta; sprinkle with mozzarella cheese. Bake 10 minutes or until cheese is melted and sauce is heated through.

Prep and cook time: 25 minutes

For a special touch, garnish with fresh basil leaves.

 **Smoked Sausage and Sauerkraut Casserole**

Makes 6 servings

> 6 fully-cooked smoked sausage links, such as German or Polish sausage (about 1½ pounds), cut into thirds
> ¼ cup packed brown sugar
> 2 tablespoons country-style Dijon mustard or German-style mustard
> 1 teaspoon caraway seeds
> ½ teaspoon dill weed
> 1 jar (32 ounces) sauerkraut, drained
> 1 small green bell pepper, stemmed, seeded and diced
> ½ cup (2 ounces) shredded Swiss cheese

1. Place sausage in large skillet with ⅓ cup water. Cover; bring to a boil over medium heat. Reduce heat to low; simmer, covered, 10 minutes. Uncover and simmer until water evaporates and sausages brown lightly.

2. While sausage is cooking, combine sugar, mustard, caraway and dill in medium saucepan; stir until blended. Add sauerkraut and bell pepper; stir until well mixed. Cook, covered, over medium heat 10 minutes or until very hot. Spoon sauerkraut into microwavable 2- to 3-quart casserole; sprinkle with cheese. Place sausage into sauerkraut; cover. Microwave on HIGH 30 seconds or until cheese melts.

Prep and cook time: 20 minutes

Easy Polenta Marinara

ACKNOWLEDGMENTS

The publisher would like to thank the companies and organizations listed below for the use of their recipes and photographs in this publication.

Birds Eye®

Del Monte Corporation

Egg Beaters® Healthy Real Egg Substitute

Fleischmann's® Spread

Grey Poupon® Mustard

Hunt-Wesson, Inc.

National Pasta Association

Walnut Marketing Board

Wesson/Peter Pan Foods Company